PERSONNEL
Today

MAKING EQUAL
OPPORTUNITIES WORK

Mary Coussey and Hilary Jackson

Pitman

Pitman Publishing
128 Long Acre, London WC2E 9AN

A Division of Longman Group UK Limited

First published in 1991

© Longman Group UK Ltd

British Library Cataloguing in Publication Data

Coussey, Mary
  Making equal opportunities work.
  I. Title II. Jackson, Hilary
  658.3
ISBN 0 273 03472 3

Printed in Great Britain by The Bath Press, Avon

Contents

FOREWORD   ix

INTRODUCTION   1
     Keeping abreast of social and economic change · Business
     benefits · Keeping up with the European Commission

CHAPTER 1   WHAT DOES EQUAL OPPORTUNITY MEAN?   4

     The legal framework · Direct and indirect
     discrimination · Positive action · **Barriers to
     equality** · Attitudes and behaviour · Search and recruitment
     methods · Spotting warning signals · Learning from
     complaints · Selection and assessment methods · Physical
     barriers · **Recognising discrimination and
     inequality** · Case study · Training points · **Checklist**

CHAPTER 2   ORGANISATIONAL STRATEGY AND STRUCTURES   17

     **Equal opportunities policy and mission
     statements** · Examples of policy statements · **Carrying out
     an Equal Opportunities Audit** · Spotting the potential for
     change · Achieving success · **Defining equal opportunities
     objectives and targets** · How to define objectives · Mission
     Statements · Targets · **Action programmes** · Sample
     action plans · Drawing up an action
     programme · **Personnel management
     structures** · Consultation · **Checklist**

CHAPTER 3   STATISTICAL MONITORING   38

     Collecting and assembling your information · Staff in
     post · Collecting information on job applicants and new
     recruits · Collecting information about people with

disabilities · Collecting ethnic origin information · Before
you start · Analysing your information; building a company
profile · Interpreting the data · Identifying where action is
needed · Action · Examples of some key barriers to
equality · **Checklist**

CHAPTER 4 IMAGE BUILDING   65

What are the barriers to applicants? · Discovering the
reasons for low application rates · Feedback from
applicants · Attracting applicants · Image building · Links
with education and careers services · Community
links · Role models · **Serving customers or clients in a
diverse labour market** · How to offer services to a diverse
community · Case study · **Checklist**

CHAPTER 5 RECRUITMENT AND SELECTION   76

Barriers to equality in selection · Sifting or screening
criteria · Qualifications and experience · The interview and
decision making · Aptitude and other selection tests · **How
to avoid bias** · Objective selection · Do-it-yourself job
analysis · Shortlisting · Objective interviewing · **Spotting
potential** · Other methods of assessing competence and
potential · Bias-free tests · Testing the test · How closely
do test results match job performance? · How to use
tests · **Checklist**

CHAPTER 6 PROMOTION AND CAREER DEVELOPMENT   93

Barriers to promotion · **Defining core skills and
experience** · Analysis of components of promotion
system · Procedures · **Performance appraisals** · Checking
appraisals for inequality · Competitive
promotion · Interviews, promotion panels and
boards · **Promotion systems** · Selection for promotion
without interview · How to identify potential · Fast-track
staff development for under-represented groups ·
Encouraging under represented groups · Case
study · **Checklist**

CHAPTER 7 EQUAL OPPORTUNITIES TRAINING   108

What is training for equal opportunities? · The
pitfalls · **Components of equality training** · Education and
awareness training · Knowledge and understanding · Skills·
Planning and setting up equal opportunities training ·

The organisational context · Training needs analysis · Some
questions to ask in identifying needs · **Training
objectives** · Line managers · Personnel staff · Line
employees · **Training content and materials** ·
Evaluation ·**Positive action/developmental training** · The
benefits of positive action training · Identifying positive
action training needs · Should the training be specific to
women, or black and Asian people? · Managing positive
action training · **Checklist**

CHAPTER 8   WORKING ARRANGEMENTS   131

Flexible working patterns · Introducing flexible working
patterns · Working out the scheme · Setting up the
scheme · **Improving parental leave arrangements and
career breaks** · Long-term career breaks · **Help with
childcare arrangements** · Choosing the right childcare
package for your organisation · Identifying demand ·
Putting together a business plan · Advantages and
disadvantages · Partnership nurseries · Workplace
nursery · Play schemes · After school care · **Checklist**

CHAPTER 9   EMPLOYING PEOPLE WITH DISABILITIES   154

Legal obligations · **Access and equipment** · **General
good practice** · Access to buildings · Equipment · A
commitment to good employment practice · Department of
Employment · Voluntary organisations · **Checklist**

CHAPTER 10   THE WORKING ENVIRONMENT   166

Dealing with complaints of discrimination · The
complaints procedure · Warning signs · **Sexual and racial
harassment** · What is harassment? · How often does
harassment occur? · Is sexual and racial harassment against
UK law? · What action can an employer take to prevent
harassment at work? · Policy statements · Complaints
procedure · Monitoring · Training · **Checklist**

CHAPTER 11   COSTS AND BENEFITS   179

Costs · Running costs · Capital costs · **Benefits** · The
ability to recruit from a wider section of the labour
market · The ability to retain staff · Improved staff
morale · Improved service delivery and client
satisfaction · **Value for money** · **Checklist**

How do industrial tribunals decide what is discriminatory? · **Race and sex discrimination law at work** · Recruitment arrangements · Access to promotion and training · Dismissals and other detriment · Part-time employees · Pregnancy and maternity leave · **Employers' liability** · Training · **Checklist**

APPENDICES
APPENDIX 1 **Cases cited: chapter 12**   195
APPENDIX 2 **Useful addresses**   197
APPENDIX 3 **Bibliography**   202

INDEX   205

Foreword

by John Banham
Director-General, Confederation of British Industry

People are central to the success of every business; they are the only source of sustainable competitive advantage. Companies which succeed have positive well-established policies for managing them.

Managers must take the lead in creating an environment where the full potential of every employee can be realised and rewarded.

The creation of a flexible, motivated workforce involves providing opportunities at all levels and in all functions, under-pinned by an equal opportunities policy. This benefits individuals and businesses and makes the best use of the skills and talents of the workforce.

The environment in which people work is of fundamental importance. Healthy and safe working surroundings mean high quality standards of protection and performance and ensure the well-being of all those in the workplace.

In addition corporate healthcare encourages healthy work and lifestyle practices. Not only are these beneficial for the individual but also contribute to lower absenteeism, improved performance and higher morale. Sickness absence alone costs British business well over £5 billion a year.

These comprehensive, practical books use the examples of a large number of companies and are designed for day-to-day use by personnel managers. Each book considers the value of the programmes, benefits to be gained, practical implementation and the costs involved.

Foreword

This book is timely. Employers are becoming increasingly aware that they can not afford to rely only on white males, who account for a little over half the labour force, to run or develop their businesses. With this growing awareness has come acceptance that equal opportunities policies are essential for good personnel management. Such policies need to focus on the barriers that prevent women, members of ethnic minorities, and people with disabilities from contributing fully to all aspects of the work of an organisation.

While some progress has undoubtedly been made on the basis of existing legislation, recent studies have shown that much remains to be done. People who are not genuinely convinced of the economic, social, and ethical case for equal opportunities can all too easily settle for complying with the absolute minimum that the law requires. But that by itself will not deliver equal opportunities in practice.

The writers recognise that if equal opportunities policies are to succeed, they must be seen as a necessary and beneficial part of good management, bringing solid advantages to the enterprises that adopt them. The best of policies are thoroughly monitored, and are only as good as the painstaking practical programmes introduced to implement them. This book establishes the sound management reasons for such policies and programmes, and provides clear step-by-step guidance for turning good intentions into practical achievements. By advocating flexibility and a tailor-made programme to suit the wide diversity of organisations, the writers show how results can be achieved in the smaller and less sophisticated concerns as well as in the most highly organised. Particularly valuable is the emphasis on the need for carefully designed training programmes for all concerned. Any policy must have support from the top, but without training targets, timetables and monitoring, there is always a danger that it may start at the top and stay there. To change attitudes is beyond the power of most organised training programmes, but changed behaviour – based on sound policies and on training – can bring about results and, over a period of time, changes in attitude.

Baroness Seear of Paddington

Introduction

What's in it for my company?

Whether in the public or private sector, whether a large organisation or a small one, it is clear from the jobs pages of any newspaper that the company of the 1990s is keen to advertise itself as an 'equal opportunity employer'. What started off in the 1970s as a marginal concern for a few local authorities has now moved centre stage for the majority of employers. And it has done so for sound economic reasons.

Making equal opportunities work for your company means:

- keeping abreast of social and economic changes;
  - getting the best out of a more diverse workforce,
- business benefits such as
  - improved service delivery and competitiveness,
  - managing change, not responding to it,
  - maintaining a better public image; and
- keeping up with developments in Europe.

Keeping abreast of social and economic change

The labour market of the 1990s looks very different from that of, say, 20 years ago. Now, almost 50% of the labour force are women, many with young children, and 4.5% of the workforce are of ethnic minority origin. A survey in 1990 estimated that 4.5% of people of working age cite a disability. The recruitment methods and working conditions that may have served well enough 20 years ago when the majority of the workforce was white and male will not be so effective in this diverse labour market. By 1995 the numbers of 16 to 24 years old in the labour market will have declined by one-fifth from the 1987 figure. But the total number in the labour market will rise by over 900,000; more than 80% of the net addition will be women returning to the labour market. And the proportion of school leavers from the ethnic minorities will increase significantly into the 1990s because the ethnic minority communities are on average younger than the population as a whole; in 1989, ethnic minorities formed 6.7% of the under-16 age group; 2% above their representation in the labour market as a whole. Further, with the coming into effect of the Single European Market, we shall have yet another source of diversity. Successful companies will be those who can innovate and manage this change.

Attitudes and expectation have changed. Young women and young people from ethnic minorities now expect to get the same jobs and career chances as young white men. They will question treatment that hinders their progress, and will work for those employers who can show that women and ethnic minorities are given the chance to get on.

So, in order to recruit and retain staff successfully in the 1990s, employers need to be more flexible and adaptable than in the past. They must learn how to sell themselves to this different labour market. And to keep staff, especially new entrants, they must get the best out of all their workforce, and have systems and conditions which allow alternative working patterns.

Business benefits

Effective equal opportunity policies have the following economic benefits:

- the most flexible and effective use of staff gives an employer a competitive edge in the labour market;
- a sound equal opportunity programme for ethnic minorities gives advantages to companies bidding for local authority contracts;
- a diverse workforce reflecting your market can result in a better informed, more adaptable organisation which is closer to customers, giving a market edge over your less responsive competitors. If the market is changing there is no sense in having white males making all the decisions;
- a thriving local community brings economic advantages to all businesses;
- managing change through effective equal opportunity programmes costs less than any changes that may be imposed.

In this book we look first at what is meant by an equal opportunity policy, then at ways of achieving change. We will work through some detailed examples of the kind of practical initiatives that form part of

MAKING EQUAL OPPORTUNITIES WORK

an equal opportunity policy, and finally examine ways of monitoring performance and measuring success.

The practice of equal opportunities is now a mainstream activity for all responsible employers. We all recognise its importance if we are to make use of our most precious national resource – the people who live in our land. Equal opportunities has a contribution to make to many of our practices: particularly recruitment, selection promotion and training.

> *Saying Yes to Equal Opportunities in Training* CTAD for the Ten Company Group, 1990

TSB ... is treating equal opportunities as a strategic issue of importance to the whole business. We recognise that we've been missing out on talent from some sections of the community, particularly the ethnic minority community ... We need to tap into that talent if we are to succeed in recruiting staff with the skills and abilities we want in the 1990s.

> Equal opportunities manager, TSB Group plc, November 1989

At the end of the day, equal opportunities is also good for business. Getting our policy right will ensure we can move with confidence into the European future of the 1990s.

> Sir John Moores CBE, The Littlewoods Organisation (*Equal Opportunities Review*, September/October 1990)

Keeping up with Europe

In the European Commission's third action programme on equal opportunities for women, covering the period 1991–5, major initiatives are proposed to promote the integration of women into the labour market. The Commission is to define the scope of equal pay for work of equal value, and clarify the scope of indirect discrimination. It will collect information about specific measures and best practice in relation to equality in the labour market. The Commission has also taken a major community-wide initiative called NOW (New Opportunities for Women), to promote vocational training and employment for women, including financial support for childcare. These initiatives and recent European Court of Justice decisions (on discrimination on grounds of pregnancy, and the Barber case on equal treatment in pension schemes for example) have a direct impact on British companies.

CHAPTER 1
What Does Equal Opportunity Mean?

Achieving equality of opportunity essentially means changing how we do things, how we behave and how one's organisation looks. It means that more women, ethnic minority and disabled applicants and employees will be given the same chances to take part, progress and succeed as white males.

The basic premise is that talent and ability is evenly spread throughout all groups and between men and women. However, women and ethnic minorities are unevenly distributed in employment, and concentrated in lower grade jobs because of the effects of past and present discriminatory practices, and of social and educational disadvantages. People with a disability are also most likely to be found in lower level jobs and this is unlikely to be entirely because of limited capacity. The long-term objective of an equal opportunity programme is to remove any barriers which prevent these groups fully taking part in an organisation, and thereby achieve a random distribution; that is a workforce which fully reflects the population at all levels.

To make sure that this happens, remedies may also have to be introduced to make up for past disadvantages, such as lack of experience or training. And it means reviewing and introducing new working patterns, to meet the changing needs of a more diverse workforce, who in turn are affected by the changing social patterns resulting from women's greater participation in work. They will begin to look for career breaks or flexible hours as dual career families increase, and both partners begin to share their domestic responsibilities.

The legal framework

The legal basis of equal opportunities at work is the 1975 Sex Discrimination Act (SDA) and the 1976 Race Relations Act (RRA). The SDA was enacted partly to bring the UK into line with the equal treatment requirements of the European Community; (Article 119 of the Treaty of Rome). The RRA was closely modelled on the SDA, and was enacted to deal with deficiencies in the earlier 1968 Act which dealt only with less favourable treatment of individuals on racial grounds. There was increasing evidence (for example see PEP: 'Racial Discrimination' 1965) that much inequality was a result of the effects of practices which excluded ethnic minority people. The need to tackle systematic discrimination, as well as individual treatment, led to the inclusion of indirect discrimination in the equality statutes.

Direct and indirect discrimination

The definitions of direct and indirect discrimination are set out in the Race Relations Act (RRA) 1976 and the Sex Discrimination Act (SDA) 1975. *Direct* discrimination means treating a person differently from other people simply because of their race, colour or ethnic origins, or because of their sex — for example, rejecting a person's application for a job, for which they have all the right qualifications and experience, simply because they are black. The law is not concerned with the motives of the person who discriminates — it is equally unlawful to discriminate as a result, for example, of pressure from other employees, or customers or because it is judged to be in the best interests of the individual woman or black person not to be offered the job as it is to discriminate as a result of personal prejudice.

Treating people in exactly the same way, however, does not necessarily avoid discrimination or achieve equality of opportunity. *Indirect* discrimination can occur even when people are treated the same. Eligibility criteria for a job or particular conditions of the job may mean that, in practice, a considerably smaller proportion of women than men, or a considerably smaller proportion of one racial group than another, can comply with the requirements. Sometimes such requirements may be necessary to carry out the job effectively, but often they are not and are simply used because 'they always have been used' or because they are convenient. (section 1(1)(b) of the SDA and RRA).

See Chapter 12, for examples of tribunal and court decisions on direct and indirect discrimination.

Positive action

Equality of opportunity is about changing the way the composition of the workforce in the organisation looks. Even if you successfully avoid direct and indirect discrimination in the way you recruit and promote people, you may not find it so easy to succeed in changing the way the organisation looks, or solve recruitment difficulties very quickly. Men and women and those from different racial groups have different educational experiences and may have experienced discrimination in previous employment so that their apparent achievements are way below their actual ability and potential. They are, in effect, starting out from further down the career ladder. In some circumstances, employers can take measures to help overcome such difficulties and give preferential treatment to one sex or a particular racial group.

The law defines the precise circumstances and the kinds of action that can be taken. The circumstances are:

(i)   where within the previous 12 months there were no persons of the sex or race in question doing that work; or

(ii) the number of persons of that sex or race doing the work is comparatively small.

The actions are:

(i)   access to facilities for training which would help fit such persons for work; and

(ii) encouragement to take advantage of opportunities for doing that work.

(section 48 of the SDA and section 37 of the RRA)

It should be stressed that taking positive action measures does not mean giving preference at the point of offering a job. It means including statements in job advertisements to encourage applicants from particular racial groups (e.g. Metropolitan Police campaign, which particularly welcomed applications from men and women from ethnic minority groups') or setting up training courses to provide people with the skills and qualifications to compete for employment in a particular kind of job.

The RRA uses the term 'racial group' for any group defined by race, colour, or ethnic or national origins or nationality. For the purposes of this book we shall use the term ethnic minority to mean people who are identifiable from appearance, speech or name, as a different race, colour or ethnic or national origin, from the majority. However, we shall concentrate on visible ethnic minorities; people whose origins are Indian, Pakistani, Bangladeshi, Chinese, African or West Indian. We concentrate on these groups because they are the most visibly identifiable as ethnic minorities; and because research has shown they suffer significantly higher levels of racial discrimination than other minorities, such as people of Greek, Polish or Italian origin.

Barriers to equality

We have defined an equal opportunities employer as one in which women, ethnic minorities and people with disabilities take part, progress and succeed in proportion to their availability in the labour market or in the workforce. We have also described the two types of discrimination recognised by the law. But removing unlawful discrimination will not be enough to achieve full participation; it will also be necessary to make up for the effects of unequal treatment in the past.

There are four main barriers to equality:

- attitudes and behaviour;
- search and recruitment methods;
- selection and assessment methods;
- physical barriers.

Attitudes and behaviour

Our attitudes and value systems are formed from our early cultural and social experiences. They can affect our judgement of people who are 'not like us'. The first step is to recognise when this is happening, before you can consider implementing training or counselling, or re-designing decision-making systems which are dealt with in detail later in the book.

Attitudes can affect behaviour in the following ways:

PREJUDICE
This is a feeling of superiority towards people from other racial groups or towards women. It is a belief that all women or people from particular groups share similar characteristics. Common generalisations are: 'women are emotional', 'women are not competitive' and 'black people are lazy'. It can also be expressed emotionally, for example because of fear or anxiety; or in negative, stereotypical language or derogatory words (such as 'Paki', 'girls', 'coloureds', 'bitch'). It is also expressed in the use of exclusionary language (e.g. using male words as universal; referring to minorities as 'them', 'these people', 'you people'). The victim group may be disparaged or caricatured; and become the butt of jokes. In formal settings women and minorities may be referred to by their first names, while white males are described as 'Mr' or by some other title; and patronised.

Examples of acts of prejudice include:

- refusing to employ minorities;

- providing them with a slower, less professional service;
- restricting minorities and women to lower status jobs;
- asking them demeaning questions;
- ignoring the contributions of women and minorities at meetings;
- actually speaking for a woman or minority;
- overemphasising 'normal' acts, perhaps over-praising or showing minorities off;
- applying different standards, accepting a white male's word but doubting that of a minority worker, or habitually clarifying or explaining their remarks.

STEREOTYPING

This involves making assumptions about the skills or behaviour of someone based on your experience of someone else from the same racial group or another woman, or on your perceptions of how women or people of that group tend to behave.

Stereotype	Comments suggesting evidence of stereotyping
Disabled staff have poor health records	'would be unable to cope with demands of the job'
Women don't want management responsibility	'would not cope with unsocial hours and working under pressure'
Afro-Caribbeans lack a business ethic	'too casual: would not adapt to our culture'
Asians prefer to work in their own business	'would not adapt to large organisation'

Stereotyping also involves the use of generalisations such as 'people like him/her...' 'they...', 'these people'.

The use of the conditional tense ('would not') suggests that the person making the comment has made an assumption about the person on the basis of a perception about how people of his or her group behave.

For more information on the existence of and dealing with stereotyping see Chapters 5 and 6 below.

CONFORMING TO PERCEIVED EMPLOYEE/CUSTOMER PREFERENCES

This involves making decisions based on your fears about how others may react because they have expressed negative views, or because you believe they will be unhelpful or unsure about working or dealing with someone who is 'not like them'.

Comments suggesting evidence of conformist discrimination

'the men won't like it'
'our customers aren't ready for women'
'our competitors haven't employed any black sales staff'
'some of our engineers are very traditional'
'the last Asian was ostracised'
'he would find it impossible to gain his staff's support'
'we can't afford to take the risk'
'she would not be able to cope with shop-floor culture'.

Again the use of the conditional term shows that the person speaking has assumed that his or her staff or customers will object to minority groups.

Indeed, even if there is evidence that staff or customers *would* object to a black or Asian person or a woman, it is unlawful to act on such pressure. In fact people are usually expressing generalised worries which do not apply when they have personal contact with someone from that group; they will relate to them as individuals. In the few cases where objections do seem real, firm action will stop it. You are merely being tested out; if you seem weak, it will encourage resistance.

For example, a high street bank manager was told by his largest account holder that the account would be withdrawn if he had to deal with a newly-appointed black cashier. The manager discussed this threat with head office and it was agreed that he should politely and firmly inform the customer that it was the bank's policy to appoint on merit, regardless of colour. The customer did not carry out his threat.

UNCONSCIOUS ASSUMPTIONS
Our attitudes about people in non-traditional roles are often unconscious, and yet can cloud our objectivity. You can see whether this is happening from looking at the language used to describe people. If there is a tendency for ethnic minorities and women to be described in terms of their appearance and manner, rather than their achievements, knowledge and skills, in comparison with white men, this is a sign that decision-makers' attitudes have affected their decisions.

Examples of comments indicating unconscious discrimination in decision-making

Women	Ethnic minorities
petite	very dark
attractive	wears beard and turban
warm	very Indian
vivacious	eager to please
pushy	aggressive/chip on shoulder
voluble	negroid features
unassertive	laid back
gentle	managed to achieve 3 'A' levels
delightful	only interested in status
bubbly personality	only interested in money
long blonde/	lacks motivation
black hair	not our type

People with disabilities	White men
'She has done well considering her disability'	has good grades
	has a clear idea of his career
'He has not let his disability affect his career'	wants to get into management
	well informed
'It was difficult to test her under pressure'	articulate
	good leader
	our type

The above comments about women and ethnic minorities are mainly concerned with their appearance, behaviour or personality, and many are negative; whereas the comments on white males are about what they have done and achieved. The comments about people with disabilities indicate surprise 'has done well' (why shouldn't they?). As isolated examples, such comments may not be significant. But if they occur with any regularity, a pattern may be building up which is evidence that different standards are being applied to white men.

CROSS-CULTURAL DIFFERENCES IN BEHAVIOUR

There are subtle rules of behaviour which vary between one organisation and another; between men and women; and between people from different ethnic groups. These differences affect our judgement of others, and can lead to discriminatory decisions.

Differences can include the following:

- degree of eye contact – either too much or too little;
- body language – e.g. use of hands and posture in chair could be either too formal or too relaxed;

- degree of directness – e.g. in describing one's achievements, and in admitting failure or claiming success – British people tend to be diffident about success, but other cultures are more open about it, which would be considered brash in Britain; also, women tend to underplay their achievements compared with men;
- degree of challenge or obstruction – e.g. in discussing hypothetical problems or views – in some cultures it is impolite to disagree with someone of a higher status;
- degree of formality – e.g. using first names or not, asking about family circumstances, and ways of 'breaking the ice';
- dress and appearance – e.g. white socks or bright tie, bright blouse/skirt, length of hair/beard, make-up and jewellery.

Being influenced in interviews by cross-cultural differences such as these indicates that selection may be biased. Besides, behaviour at interview is a poor indicator of performance and using information about behaviour at interview to assess skills, achievements and motivation can be very misleading and inaccurate. Further, behaviour at interview is an interaction between people, and our own personal feelings affect what we ask. For example, if you have decided that someone is 'shifty', you will feel uneasy with them, and look for information which reinforces that feeling.

Look out for any comments on appearance, dress or personal mannerisms which may indicate bias.

Search and recruitment methods

Many traditional recruitment methods tend to be a channel for attracting only one kind of applicant. If this happens, you will be excluding good quality people from minority groups, people with disabilities, and women. If your company or department is seen as all-white and male, it will take some work to change this image and persuade people from other groups to apply to your company.

Traditional recruitment methods include the following.

- Word of mouth referrals from your staff which tend to replicate the pattern of your workforce. If women, particular minorities or people with disabilities are not applying, check where your recruits are learning about vacancies.
- Relying on casual callers may replicate the make-up of your locality. It may also cut down applications from people with disabilities if access to your particular office is difficult.
- Using selected job centres, employment agencies or schools careers services may restrict your choice of applicants. They

also tend to refer 'marketable' people and may assume that you do not want ethnic minorities or women. Ask agencies why no minorities have been sent.

- Advertisements, recruitment literature and your company image may project an unwelcoming company or a white male image. Check the numbers of each group who apply for jobs. This will tell you whether you are attracting people from all the available labour market. In Chapter 4 you will find out how to build up your image.

Selection and assessment methods

There are two ways in which selection can exclude certain groups of applicants. Each time people are compared with each other or against a standard criterion there is scope for discrimination. In the past, selection favoured white males. The selection standards will be based on the employers' experience of the best performers, and a preference for white males may be unintentionally built into the process. For example, a preference for certain qualifications or level of experience will tend to exclude women and ethnic minority people with ability, because they have usually followed a different career route. Aptitude tests and interviews may also favour one group.

To check whether this happens in your organisation, look at the numbers who are screened in, and see whether there is a pattern favouring one particular group.

PROMOTION AND DEVELOPMENT

The same processes occur in promotion and performance appraisal systems. Seniority, testing and bias in performance assessment may, in practice, favour white males. Often this goes back to access to training and fast track development, which in its turn may be restricted to white males.

Physical barriers

There are strong, unwritten rules about working patterns. In many organisations it is expected that managers will show their commitment to the company by working long hours, or by attending out-of-hours functions (whether formal, or by the informal 'pub' or 'club' culture), or by attending weekend or evening training events. But, many of these requirements add little to work output or individual effectiveness. They owe more to the need for people to have social networks, or they may be long-established working patterns and no one has ever questioned the need for them.

Talk to some male senior managers about what influences their choice in promoting or posting staff. Do they overlook women who are not part of the 'long hours' culture? If so, you need to have a spelled-out policy making it clear that your company will not overload anyone who has worked part-time or shorter hours.

Consider whether or not you can offer part-time senior level jobs, or more flexible office hours (with some work or short-term projects which can be done from home). For further information see Chapter 8.

Recognising discrimination and inequality in your organisation

An understanding of the nature of racial and sexual discrimination, and of the processes which cause inequality, is essential. Employers must know what to look for; how to evaluate the facts about behaviour and practices discussed above; and how to deal with discrimination and find solutions without causing defensive reactions.

Spotting warning signals

Carry out spot checks of your recruitment or promotion panels, or have a look at a sample of appraisal or job performance forms. About 50 decisions will give you a feel for what is going on. Look out for a pattern of discriminatory comments, as in the examples above. Is there a pattern of decisions in favour of one group – for example, white males? If so, you need to implement a more objective selection, training and counselling programme. See Chapters 5 to 7.

Learning from complaints

There are many lessons to be learned from evaluating what has gone wrong in any conflict or decision which results in a complaint. Normally when a complaint is made, everyone takes up a defensive position and justifies their actions. An organisation normally defends its managers. The best way to learn the lessons from studying events leading to a complaint is to analyse them without judging. You may find something along the following lines:

- the complainant's grievance was ignored or trivialised;
- racist or sexist behaviour was overlooked or seen as irrelevant;
- the grievance procedure was too slow and formal to resolve the break down in inter-personal relationships;
- the complainant becomes very angry and determined, but isolated;

- the matter becomes intractable or insoluble;
- feelings are hurt and positions entrenched.

DEALING WITH COMPLAINTS

From an analysis of complaints such as these it will be seen that it is much easier to resolve allegations of racism or sexism if they are considered promptly and informally with counselling or prompt action. Make sure that everyone has a contact point at which to raise a grievance and that everyone knows the name of his or her contact.

Managers or specialist personnel staff need to be skilled in interviewing, counselling and able to give negative feedback non-judgementally; and be aware and take into account the subtleties of inter-cultural and sexist perceptions. Any skilled counsellor or specialist equal opportunity officer is best used as an independent resource and evaluator.

Avoid getting into industrial tribunals. Aim to resolve the grievance by counselling. Do not be afraid to admit mistakes. Your credibility as an equal opportunity employer will gain little from fighting complaints. And make sure that the lessons learned from individual cases are fed back into manager training. See Chapter 10 for more information about dealing with complaints and Chapter 12 for examples of the law in practice.

If your company has adopted an equal opportunity programme and is successfully raising awareness of discrimination, you will probably find an increase in the numbers of staff willing to complain about discrimination. This is normal: staff feel more confident about raising such issues and have higher expectations. Be prepared by making sure that you have trained counsellors and trained managers available with the skills to resolve disputes and manage diversity.

CASE STUDY – Marilyn Ross

Marilyn Ross was a black woman who worked in the claims department of an insurance company. She complained to the personnel officer that her manager would not let her work on big commercial cases. She was confined to small-scale domestic claims, restricting her experience and reducing her promotion chances. She complained to her departmental manager, who looked into the matter, and said he could find no evidence of racial or sex discrimination; she simply lacked the experience for commercial claims work. He acknowledged that her colleagues had made adverse comments about mixed marriages and immigrants, but felt that this was not intended to be offensive, and had nothing to do with her complaint about job allocation.

The personnel officer discussed Ms Ross's complaint with her line manager. He was unwilling to trust her on commercial claims because he knew she had friends working for one of his major clients. There were concerns that she might not be objective or rigorous about any claims that this client might make. He knew about the alleged comments by colleagues, but felt these had not been relevant: they were 'office banter'.

The question of Marilyn's contacts with a client had never been discussed with her; nor had he said anything to her colleagues about their comments. The personnel officer's advice was that Ms Ross should be transferred to commercial work with her duties defined and be given training. The possible conflict of interests should be openly discussed and the confidentiality rules explained. His staff should be consulted about avoiding insensitive racist comments.

Training points:

- managers should avoid making assumptions and should discuss their concerns with staff direct;
- all staff should be given the same chances for work allocation;
- office banter may be hurtful to someone with different perceptions and, if ignored this will rankle. Speak to the offenders quickly and give them any feedback.

- look for evidence from comments, inconsistencies of treatment and from patterns in decision-making that favour one group, which suggests that attitudes may be affecting manager-behaviour;
- carry out spot checks of decisions to check against these factors;
- analyse what has gone wrong in a conflict or complaint, and make sure everyone learns from any mistakes;
- check your recruitment and selection methods for evidence of indirect discrimination;
- question assumptions about working patterns;
- take a firm line against racist or sexist banter; it can never be acceptable.

MAKING EQUAL OPPORTUNITIES WORK

CHAPTER 2
Organisational Strategy and Structures

In this chapter we look at Equal Opportunity Policy Statements, and how to carry out an equal opportunities audit to focus efforts and ensure best use of resources. Spotting potential for change and finding allies is also important, and we concentrate on starting in a small way and building on your success. Objectives, targets and accountability are dealt with and finally action programmes and personnel management structures.

Equal opportunities policy and mission statements

Many companies, especially those having formal joint consultative procedures with trade unions, have found it useful to have an agreed policy statement setting out the basis of their equal opportunity policy. These statements are a useful starting point for defining a programme of action and objectives for achieving equal opportunities. But they must never become a substitute for action.

A policy statement is useful for the following reasons. It will:

- define the basis for your policy;
- define the scope of your policy;
- give a signal to all staff that the company is changing;
- give an opportunity to demonstrate top-level support for the policy;
- give an opportunity to show widespread backing for the policy from trade unions;
- provide a focus for taking action.

A policy should be no more than a broad statement of intent and an expression of priorities. Do not include long statements of desirable intentions which cannot be carried out, otherwise your policy will lack credibility. For example, a policy may include avoiding discrimination on the basis of social class. This may be a worthwhile intention, but cannot realistically be acted upon.

Your policy should be backed up by a specific programme of action and measurable objectives. If you cannot include any specific action to support one of your policy aims, it is best to exclude that aim. If there is strong support in your company for including particular groups which have no legislative basis of protection, such as sexual orientation, the most appropriate place to include it would be as a ground for involving the grievance procedure, rather than in a policy statement which is otherwise all-embracing.

Examples of policy statements

TSB GROUP
"Statement
To achieve our business objectives the TSB Group is committed to provide equal opportunities in employment and customer service.

The best person for the job
We shall recruit and develop staff on the basis of the suitability of their skills and experience for the job.

The best in customer service
We shall provide a non-discriminatory, high standard of service to all our customers and clients. Decisions will be made only on the basis of actuarial or financial considerations."

LEICESTER CITY COUNCIL
The Council's Policy Statement

"(a) The City Council is committed to:
  (i)   positive action to promote equality of opportunity in employment; and
  (ii) regular, comprehensive monitoring of the results of this commitment.
 (b) All employees and applicants for employment will be given equal opportunity in recruitment, in training and in promotion to more senior jobs, irrespective of their racial origins, sex, disability, marital status, religious beliefs, social background or sexual orientation.
 (c) All other policies and practices associated with the Council's role as an employer must be applied with strict observance of the equal opportunity policy and philosophy. This also applies

to training opportunities except in those cases where the Council intends to take positive action to provide special training for particular disadvantaged groups.

(d) The City Council will take steps to utilise those statutory provisions which permit special action to be taken to improve recruitment to work where disadvantaged groups are under-represented.

(e) Employees are expected to behave in a non-racist and non-sexist way towards both the public and fellow employees. Any breach of the policy may result in the disciplinary procedure being invoked. Where circumstances are appropriate disciplinary action, up to, and including dismissal may result."

FORD MOTOR COMPANY

"Joint statement of equal opportunity
Statement signed by the company and its trade unions representing salaried and hourly-paid employees.

1. Commitment to equal opportunity

1.1 The company and the trade unions are committed to the principle of equal opportunity in employment. The company and the trade unions declare their opposition to any form of less favourable treatment, whether through direct or indirect discrimination accorded to employees and applicants for employment on the grounds of race, religious beliefs, creed, colour, nationality, ethnic or national origins, marital/parental status or sex.

1.2 The company and the trade unions similarly declare their opposition to any form of less favourable treatment accorded to employees and applicants for employment on the grounds of non-job-related handicaps and unfair discrimination on grounds of age.

1.3 The company and the trade unions recognise their obligations under the Sex Discrimination Act 1975 and the Race Relations Act 1976 and support the spirit and intent of the related Codes of Practice:

for the elimination of discrimination on the grounds of sex and marriage and the promotion of equality of opportunity in employment;

for the elimination of racial discrimination and the promotion of equality of opportunity in employment.

2. Employment practices

2.1 The company and the trade unions state their wholehearted support for the principles and practice of equal opportunity and agree that it is the duty of all employees to accept their personal responsibility for fostering a fully integrated community at work by adhering to the principles of equal opportunity and maintaining racial harmony. The company will, therefore, actively promote equal opportunity through the application of employment policies which will ensure that individuals receive treatment which is fair, equitable and consistent with their relevant aptitudes, potential, skills and abilities. The trade unions will seek to ensure that all members and representatives comply with these principles and practices.

2.2 The company will ensure that individuals are recruited and selected, promoted and treated on objective criteria having regard to relevant aptitudes, potential, skills and abilities. In particular, no applicant or employee will be placed at a disadvantage by requirements or conditions which are not necessary to the performance of the job or which constitute indirect unfair discrimination.

2.3 The company and the trade unions recognise the problems that sexual harassment may cause in the workplace and are jointly committed to ensuring that such unacceptable behaviour does not take place. Sexual harassment includes unwanted physical contact; suggestive remarks or behaviour; compromising invitations; demands for sexual favours and similar unwanted behaviour. Sexual harassment is regarded as unfair discriminatory conduct and will be dealt with in accordance with procedures set out in 4.2 below.

3. Monitoring and review arrangements

3.1 The company and the trade unions recognise that regular monitoring of the ethnic origin and sex of employees is essential to the thorough review of the effectiveness of the joint statement and to this end the company will maintain and improve as necessary, the current equal opportunity monitoring arrangements. These may be extended where agreed by the company and trade unions for the purpose of completing jointly agreed special exercises at local or national level.

3.2 The successful implementation of this joint statement is dependent on the regular examination of progress towards equal opportunity and the development of local initiatives. To this end, local management and trade unions are expected to set up appropriate joint bodies at plant or equivalent level.

3.3 The company will send a copy of the company-wide annual review of equal opportunity statistics to the trade unions.

3.4 The practical application of this joint statement will be subject to regular review at national level to ensure that it continues to be fully effective.

4. Grievance and disciplinary procedures

4.1 The company and trade unions will ensure that individual employees or groups of employees who believe they have experienced direct or indirect discrimination are properly represented. Any employee who feels that he or she has been treated unfairly in connection with his or her employment should raise his or her grievance through the appropriate procedure when every effort will be made to secure a satisfactory resolution. In addition, both the company and the trade unions will ensure that any employees making a complaint of unfair discrimination will be protected from victimisation.

4.2 The company will continue to treat unfair discriminatory conduct by any employee as a disciplinary offence.

5. Training and advertising

5.1 The company will provide in agreement with the trade unions, suitable and relevant equal opportunity training, as necessary and on a jointly agreed syllabus, for employees and trade union representatives. The trade unions agree to support and participate in such training programmes and to encourage their representatives to attend where appropriate. These arrangements in no way preclude the separate provision of training by the company or the trade unions to meet particular needs.

5.2 When vacancies are advertised, the company will continue to ensure such advertising, both in placement and content, is compatible with the terms of this joint statement. To this end, opportunities will be taken, through language, images or declarations, as appropriate, to show that the company is an equal opportunity employer.

6. Communications

6.1 The company and the trade unions undertake to bring the principles set out above to the attention of all employees and trade union representatives."

Carrying out an equal opportunities audit

Many countless factors, such as attitudes and values, competing priorities, entrenched processes and lack of a clear strategy and objectives all affect the capacity of an organisation to change. No manager can deal with all these factors, and an equal opportunity programme that attempts to do so without first carrying out a stock-take or audit, to identify clear goals and timetables, will be unworkable.

To get results from a policy, it is necessary to identify as specifically as possible, the following issues.

- What would produce the quickest results in reducing gaps and changing levels at which men/women, white/ethnic minorities or disabled are employed?
- What are the biggest gaps in progress?
- Where is the greatest risk of discrimination and complaints?
- What are the reasons for the inequality? Is there scope for changing behaviour or practices? Are there alternatives or remedies?
- What other pressures for change are there?
- Is there support for change at senior level?
- Will the change help to solve any other problems?

Once you have identified as many of the above factors as possible, this is the place to start.

Spotting the potential for change

You will need to obtain information from your staff both by observation and discussions, and in large organisations, by commissioning a survey to identify:

- where technology, working patterns or the workforce is changing;
- who 'owns' the problem and who wants to take the lead in solving it;
- the possible consequences of change – who else will be affected or may be able to control the policy;
- the organisational context – who controls resources or delegates authority;
- who is likely to resist.

Achieving success

It is important to show early results from your equal opportunity programme, so that staff can see the benefits for themselves. It will also give the programme credibility. In too many companies, equal opportunities is experienced as a paper-producing matter, and statements of intent are not translated into action.

The best way to achieve results is to

- identify potential for change (see above);
- find allies: staff with an interest in managing change for other reasons, such as an ageing work force, high turnover or a need to retain skills or introduce new skills and ideas;
- start in a small way and make sure you really control what is to be done, and the resources to be allocated;
- identify all the variables involved. Make sure that they can be changed.

Then develop your plan with your staff through education; explain your aims to them and get their involvement in solving the problem. Listen to and resolve any anxieties they may have. Then define the tasks to be done, making a clear decision on what is to be done by what date and by whom.

Afterwards, evaluate the success of your intervention and identify those factors which were effective in planning and operations (Chapter 3 deals with monitoring methods in detail). Then list these lessons to persuade others of the benefits of equal opportunity interventions. Offer to produce a 'tool kit' for other managers based on your experience.

Defining equal opportunities objectives and targets

Many employers have found it necessary to build on their policy statements and define what they expect from their policies, since there is a wide variety of perceptions about equal opportunities. But everyone needs to be working to the same definition towards specific measurable and realistic objectives.

The following may be indications that policy statements are unconvincing or unclear:

- managers complain that standards are being lowered;
- managers complain that they can no longer take decisions, 'everything is illegal';
- employees complain of 'reverse discrimination or positive discrimination' and resent the policy;
- women and ethnic minorities do not believe in your policy statements;
- women and ethnic minorities still do not apply for jobs and promotion;
- incidents between employees from different racial groups, or complaints of inequality or harassment become major confrontations or end in an industrial tribunal;

- the policy is mocked or trivialised;
- results are not being achieved.

How to define objectives

These problems will, of course, not all be solved simply by setting clear objectives. They also suggest that you have training and communication needs. But the process of defining and setting objectives allows managers to discuss their anxieties, helps to allay misconceptions and clarifies ideas.

The kinds of objectives and targets your organisation might adopt include the following:

- a group or company mission statement and objectives;
- target dates for the completion of particular projects or programmes of work; and
- numerical targets reflecting the way in which you expect the organisation to look in, say, five years time (see Chapter 3).

Mission statements

A mission statement is essentially a policy statement, but where a policy statement takes as its starting point the particular policy in question – an equal opportunity policy – and states what the policy is intended to achieve and how it will work, a mission statement takes as its starting point the overall aims and objectives of the organisation, and sets out how and why the particular policy is important to these overall objectives. In other words, a mission statement places the organisation's equal opportunity policy firmly in the mainstream of the organisation's overall objectives.

These objectives for equal opportunities programmes must be clear, precise, realistic, achievable and measurable. They must also apply to each level of management, from the group or company as a whole to the individuals within the company.

GROUP OR COMPANY OBJECTIVES

"We aim to balance the company workforce by the 1990s. By balanced workforce we mean achieving and maintaining equitable representation of all employee groups – majority females, majority males, minority females, minority males – in all grade bands, in all functions and organisations."

(Xerox quoted in *Promoting minorities and women*, published by BNA, Washington 1990).

"Network television, network radio, and news and current affairs will aim to reflect the ethnic composition of the nation they serve; regional broadcasting to reflect the ethnic composition of their local communities."

BBC News Release, August 1989

These objectives define a measurable outcome – 'equitable representation' 'reflect the composition of the nation...', and specify where they should be carried out ('all grade bands'...'Network Television...'), but in broad terms they would also be suitable for a group or corporate statement.

DEPARTMENTAL ACCOUNTABILITY

In a large company, and particularly a company with a number of separate sites, separate mission statements for separate departments may be needed. Departmental objectives can be tied into the company's overall objectives, but adopting departmental objectives in this way can be made more relevant to the work of staff in a department and will therefore encourage understanding and ownership. The use of staff discussion groups can help to generate understanding and ideas for departmental action plans.

If your organisation already has a departmental system of accountability, you can tie accountability for equal opportunity policies into this and into the budgetary arrangements. If you have a 'departmental' equal opportunity officer (see 'Personnel management structures' section, below), it makes sense to ensure accountability at departmental level.

Departmental objectives can also provide an opportunity to try different approaches tailor-made for different parts of the organisation; and they can encourage different parts of the organisation to 'learn' from each other. Further, accountability at this level enables the company to build in a 'reward system' to encourage further action to achieve greater equality. The Department of Employment, for example, operates a 'Fit for Work' scheme. It operates on a national basis and there is an annual award system that marks those companies that have been particularly effective in providing employment opportunities for people with disabilities. A similar scheme could be operated within your own organisation at a departmental level and across the range of equal opportunity issues.

INDIVIDUAL ACCOUNTABILITY

An effective equal opportunity policy means instituting change throughout the organisation, affecting the decisions and behaviour of everyone in the organisation, particularly every manager. Decisions and behaviour can be changed through training, through introducing new procedures, through setting standards and by ensuring that people are accountable for their behaviour.

One way of achieving personal accountability and responsibility among individual staff for equal opportunity policies is to build this into any annual staff appraisal system that your organisation operates. In a large organisation, this may be a formal, written appraisal, while in smaller organisations, it may simply take the form of an oral interview. In each case, you can take account of the company's equal opportunity policies during the appraisal process.

In the case of a written appraisal system, you could:

- include on the appraisal form, the company's equal opportunity statement in order to highlight both to the member of staff who is being assessed and the manager who is undertaking the assessment, that equal opportunities are a key consideration;
- set equal opportunity objectives for each member of staff. It is common for staff appraisal systems not only to assess performance retrospectively, but also to set performance objectives for the coming year. Managers should also set objectives for their staff in consultation with them which focus on the equal opportunity aspects of their work. This will encourage staff to take action in support of the company's policies. It will also encourage them to think about how their actions can contribute, or fail to contribute, to achieving greater equality of opportunity;
- ensure that the general criteria against which performance is assessed takes account of equal opportunity issues. Formal appraisal systems will usually set the general criteria against which performance is to be assessed; for example, management skills, work output, written and oral communication etc. Inclusion of an equal opportunity criterion will mark its importance. Staff and managers will have to look at their work and responsibilities from this perspective. How you do this will depend on the nature of your organisation, the nature of the work that is undertaken and the nature of the appraisal system. For example, you might include a general criterion that assesses what the individual has done to support and further the company's equal opportunity policies, or you might modify the criteria against which management skills are measured to take account of the extent to which staff reflect the principle of equality in their performance in this area.

Some staff appraisal objectives:

1. 'to ensure that all relevant recruitment literature is translated into Punjabi, Urdu etc.' (member of staff with recruitment responsibilities);
2. 'hold a discussion group with all the black and Asian staff or staff with disabilities, to identify any special needs and to obtain feedback about the effectiveness of the company's equal opportunity policy' (staff manager);
3. 'to undertake a survey of staff to identify childcare needs' (personnel manager or staff manager of large command);
4. 'to ensure that all my staff are aware of and understand the aims of the company's equal opportunity policy' (staff manager);
5. 'to review working arrangements to identify how flexible working patterns might most effectively be introduced' (staff manager);
6. 'to attend an equal opportunities training course to obtain a better understanding of disability at work and the availability of equipment to help overcome any special needs' (all members of staff);
7. 'to ensure that women are nominated for training at the same rate as men' (TSB 1990; departmental objective);
8. 'to nominate five women and two ethnic minority staff for management training by 1992 and ensure their necessary career development to prepare them';
9. 'to set up a sectional review of clerical recruitment, to improve links with local communities';
10. 'to plan for and implement the company "return to work scheme" for the division by the end of the year'.

The same elements of equal opportunity objectives and performance measurement can be reflected in a more informal, oral appraisal system. This is best achieved through guidance on the way in which such appraisals should be carried out and by ensuring that equal opportunity objectives are set at departmental or divisional level.

Targets

A planned equal opportunities programme is an essential part of any equal opportunity policy. It is, however, likely to be more effective if this programme can be tied into the organisation's overall plans and policies. For example, a move to new premises by your organisation would provide a good opportunity to tackle such matters as access to the building for people with disabilities, or the provision of childcare facilities, and it would clearly be sensible in planning your equal opportunity programme to take account of any such plans in setting your priorities and a timetable for action. More generally, many organisations are now adopting 'human resource development' plans and equal opportunity programmes are a key part of human resource development. Making sure that equal opportunity objectives are included in your organisation's development plan and that your equal opportunity action programme takes account of actions that are planned as part of the human resource development plan will also be helpful. It will, for example:

- help to achieve support and commitment from personnel staff for your equal opportunity programme;
- help to set priorities for action;
- provide an agreed framework for a regular annual report on progress;
- give a high profile to the organisation's equal opportunity programme; and
- avoid any conflict or duplication between the two programmes.

NUMERICAL TARGETS

There is nothing new about the idea of setting numerical targets. It is a well-established method of achieving both quantity and quality control in manufacturing, of achieving financial objectives or of achieving change more generally. For example, a production target might be set in order to ensure a reject rate of no more than 1%. The government sets targets for a minimum rate of inflation, a minimum level of increase in wages and a minimum reduction in public expenditure. Numerical targets might be set for wider policy changes such as the promotion of a new image for the organisation. For example, you might aim, by the end of the year, to have revamped the decor of a minimum number of retail outlets, recruited x number of new shop managers with a particular kind of experience and changed the age profile of the people who shop with you to an average age of x years etc. In each of these cases, targets are set for specific areas of activity which contribute to the overall policy objective. They provide a goal to aim for and benchmarks against which to measure progress. They are not quotas or ends in themselves. If the government sets a target for a minimum of 5% inflation by the end of the year, it is not ruling out the possibility or desirability of a 4% rate of inflation. It is simply saying that the rate of inflation is a key element of achieving the overall objective of a more stable economy and that, given current circumstances, achieving a 5% rate of inflation by the end of the year seems feasible and desirable. Numerical targets of this kind can help identify key areas where change is necessary to achieve the overall policy objective and help people to measure the size of the change that is needed. It can provide a benchmark against which to measure performance and demonstrate that change is being achieved.

The kind of numerical targets you might set for your equal opportunity programme are as follows.

- *Recruitment targets* A minimum of x% of all new recruits of ethnic minority origin, representing the representation in the workforce as a whole by 1992; an increase in applications from people with disabilities of x%; an increase of x% in the number of recruitment panels which are chaired by or include women members; women to represent x% of science students sponsored through university.
- *Promotion targets* Minimum of x% of promotees to be people with a disability; a minimum of x% of managers at level A in the organisation to be people of ethnic minority origin; at least one woman at top management level by 1995; an increase of x% in the number of people of ethnic minority origin represented on promotion panels.
- *Working patterns* x% of posts across the organisation to be available on a part-time or job-share basis by 1995; all requests for flexible working patterns to be met; x number of sheltered placements for people with severe disabilities by 1993; three workplace nurseries to be established by 1995;
- *Training* All top and senior managers to have participated in two days equal opportunity training by the end of the year; x% of those appointed as staff trainers to be of ethnic minority origin; all staff in the organisation to have attended a one-day equal opportunity training course by 1993.

Action programmes

If your company has accepted the need for a company-wide strategy to develop an equality programme, then your priority tasks will be easier to define. But you will need to carry out the analysis and planning described earlier in this chapter in order to identify priority tasks and completion dates. This will determine your action programme, and the targets and timetables to be included.

Sample action plans

TSB GROUP

Action	Completion date
1.0 Recruitment and selection	
1.1 Provide selection training for all line managers who recruit	March 1991
1.2 Review content of advertisements	Ongoing
1.3 Develop appropriate wording to go in all external advertisements to emphasise the positive attitude of GHO towards training and development after recruitment	January 1991
1.4 Review application form	January 1991
2.0 Promotion and training	
2.1 In revamped GHO training programme to be issued early 1991, include modules for women's development	March 1991
3.0 Review of appraisal training	
3.1 Continue implementation of Career Development meetings with senior and middle management	Ongoing
4.0 Discipline and grievance	
4.1 Revise procedures to include discrimination, harassment and victimisation, to be published in revised GHO Staff Manual	January 1991
5.0 Domestic responsibilities	
5.1 Review maternity arrangements and benefits	March 1991
5.2 Review pro-rata conditions for part time staff	March 1991
5.3 Examine family leave package	September 1991
5.4 Introduce paternity leave	November 1991
6.0 Job evaluation	
6.1 Revised scheme installed, ensuring best practice and fair application, with the meeting of up-to-date legal requirements on equal pay for work of equal value	December 1990
7.0 Management of equal opportunities	
7.1 Establish Equal Opportunities Steering Group	January 1991
7.2 Complete Equal Opportunities training for Directors and Team Leaders	March 1991
7.3 Integrate equal opportunities into management training	June 1991

MAKING EQUAL OPPORTUNITIES WORK

Action	Completion date
7.4 Integrate equal opportunities in induction training	January 1991
7.5 Include updated policy statement in revised Staff Manual for GHO	November 1990
7.6 Equal Opportunities policy statements to be issued as Staff Notices	December 1990

LITTLEWOODS' EQUAL OPPORTUNITIES CODE OF PRACTICE

Responsibilities of managers and supervisors

The success of our equal opportunities programme depends on the managers and supervisors at all levels in the company. They must be made aware of what is expected of them by the company and what is required of them by law; and given continuous training and support.

Check that:

- All managers and supervisors are briefed on their responsibilities and supported by regular training.
- Managers at all levels are aware of the equal opportunities performance of their subordinate managers and supervisors, and that assessment of that performance is included in the annual performance appraisal.
- All managers who are responsible for selecting employees for training or for allocating work ensure that no discrimination is made, either directly or indirectly. All employees are to be given equal access to training, further education, personal development, and increased job satisfaction, regardless of gender, marital status, race or disability.
- All managers and supervisors take positive steps to enable the recruitment of traditionally disadvantaged groups and to assist them to qualify for available job openings.
- Managers promote equal opportunities to their staff and encourage people of both sexes and different races to work together and eliminate discrimination.
- Managers are aware that equal opportunities managers are available for consultation and advice.

Training

Training is a basic tool in achieving equal opportunities within our organisation. Its main use in this respect is to redress imbalances in staffing identified by the yearly review which is part of our equal opportunities action programme. If, for example, it is shown that a particular type of job is being done entirely or mainly by either men or women, or if in any division or specific type of job the proportion of black people or people of ethnic minority origin is low, we will provide, and are legally allowed to do so, training facilities for members of the minority group concerned.

Check that:

- A session on equal opportunities is included in all induction programmes.
- The equal opportunities training programme provides all staff with a training or personnel function with the knowledge, skills and awareness necessary to operate the legislation, company policy and code of practice.
- Female employees are identified for inclusion in accelerated management development programmes.
- Women, black people, ethnic minority groups and disabled people have access to all measures which ensure fair recruitment and career progression.
- Training is offered to groups of people who are under-represented, either in a particular job or at certain levels within the company, in accordance with the positive discrimination measures allowed under s.47 of the Sex Discrimination Act and s.37 of the Race Relations Act.
- Appropriate additional training (for example on changes in technology) is made available to women returning to work after maternity leave or after a longer break to rear children.
- Statistical analysis of the employment of women, black people and ethnic minority groups is monitored quarterly.
- Divisional staffing targets, including those set for the progression of women, black people, ethnic minority groups and disabled people, are reviewed annually.

It is our policy to provide training for any employee who needs or will benefit from it. Language courses for members of ethnic minority groups with limited knowledge of English, additional training courses for women returning to work after a period of absence are examples of the assistance we will provide to employees who are disadvantaged in any way.

Check that:

- Language courses are offered to members of ethnic minority groups whose limited knowledge of English restricts them as to the type of work they can do.

- If staff with domestic responsibilities are selected for residential training courses, adequate notice is given to enable them to make necessary domestic arrangements, e.g. childcare.
- Consideration is given to the provision of childcare facilities if the parent responsible for the children is selected for a residential course.

Drawing up an action programme

Step one
Planning
define tasks
allocate tasks
agree/decide dates

Step two
Analysis
review data on workforce
review data on labour market
identify gaps – identify starting point
review systems and
management priorities

Step three
Solutions
define objectives – consult and agree
define changes
define and allocate task
and timetables
define targets and timetables – issue action programme
measure performance and evaluate
identify lessons and review/
adjust solutions

Personnel management structures

It is important to have a clear structure for implementing an equal opportunities programme. The main objectives are to ensure that the programme has a sufficiently high profile, that resources are allocated to achieve progress, and that the policy and programme are understood by and involve all those working in the organisation, particularly key people such as personnel managers, trainers, trade unions, women, ethnic minorities and people with disabilities.

The right structure will depend on the nature of your organisation. Here are some examples of arrangements that could be adopted.

You will need to establish a system of responsibilities within your personnel management structure. You should consider the following models.

- Appoint full-time corporate and divisional equal opportunity officers (this is a model that has been adopted by local authorities and by other major employers such as the BBC).
- Nominate posts within the personnel management function, both centrally and at regional/divisional level, to have primary responsibility for equal opportunity policies. The post-holder may have the title of equal opportunity officer, but with a wider range of personnel management responsibilities (this is a model that has been adopted by the civil service and by employers such as BP).
- Adopt a more integrated approach in which there is no nominated equal opportunity officer and instead equal opportunity responsibilities are built into the job descriptions of all personnel managers and trainers etc.

Each of these models has its advantages and disadvantages. The first ensures a high profile for the company's equal opportunity policies and ensures that the post-holder does not have competing demands on his or her time. The disadvantages are that equal opportunity policies can become marginalised and, if the equal opportunity officer is not at a senior enough level, he or she can be excluded from decision-making.

The second model also offers a high profile for the company's policies. Making use of existing posts and structures also helps ensure that the equal opportunity officer is not forgotten and is regularly involved in decision-making. Having other personnel management responsibilities can also be directly helpful. An equal opportunity officer who, for example, is also responsible for training will be able to take equal opportunity training initiatives more easily and quickly than if he or she is reliant on someone else to take action. The disadvantage is of course that the equal opportunity officer may find so many competing demands on his or her time that is it difficult to give the attention needed to equal opportunities. So you must make sure that the equal opportunity officer has available enough staff resources and time.

The third model offers the greatest scope to ensure that equal opportunity policies are, from the beginning, integrated into mainstream management practice. However, in the early stages of implementing an equal opportunity policy, the absence of an equal opportunity officer to act as a catalyst may mean that progress is slower, that equal opportunity policies become no one's priority and that people are unclear about what they should be doing and are ill-equipped to carry it out. The kind of integrated approach in this model requires a particularly effective system of objective setting, accountability and annual monitoring.

In practice, most organisations need an equal opportunity officer (whether the first or second model) to co-ordinate and take a lead in implementing the company's policy. Where organisations are large and have a divisional or local structure, it can also be an advantage to have regional or local equal opportunity officers. One of the keys to the success of both these models is the person who is appointed as equal opportunity officer. A good equal opportunity officer will need the following skills and attributes:

- to be at a senior enough level in the organisation to be able to have influence in the decision-making process;
- to have the confidence of top management, other personnel colleagues and staff in general, particularly women, ethnic minorities and people with disabilities;
- to have an understanding of equal opportunity issues and the way discrimination can occur;
- to have experience of personnel management issues more generally;
- to have good inter-personal communication and negotiating skills;
- to be persuasive, resourceful, creative and determined.

Consultation

If getting the right management structure for implementing your company's equal opportunity policies is important, so is setting up the right structures to ensure proper consultation with staff and trade unions. Again, having the right structures will depend on the nature of your organisation and, in this case, the way in which your trade unions choose to organise themselves. But proper consultation will be invaluable in helping to implement your equal opportunity policies effectively. Consultation with trade unions, or with staff associations as appropriate, can be helpful in:

- communicating the policy and its objectives;
- allaying any fears and concerns that staff may have about such initiatives as ethnic origin monitoring;
- achieving full co-operation with the support for the company's policies; and
- providing ideas and help in implementing the policies.

You will find it helpful to set up a special management/trade union equal opportunities committee to monitor progress, develop ideas and agree a plan of action or discuss such matters on a regular basis within the context of an existing personnel management committee.

Consultation with black and Asian people, people with disabilities and women is also important. This can be achieved in a number of ways. Women's groups or pressure groups may already exist within your organisation or within your trade unions. Alternatively, you may choose to hold *ad hoc* meetings of women, people with disabilities or ethnic minority staff to explore issues with them or you may choose to co-opt individual representatives on to a management/trade union joint committee. Ensuring that ethnic minorities, women and people with disabilities are represented among those working as equal opportunity staff should also be a priority.

┌─ *CHECKLIST* ──

- define your policy clearly to set the scene and signal a start to action;
- carry out an audit to identify priority areas for action;
- define specific company, departmental and individual measurable objectives so that all your managers know what they need to do, by when;
- make sure accountability for meeting individual objectives is included in your company's appraisal and reward system;
- include numerical targets in your objectives as benchmarks for measuring progress;
- make sure you have a clear structure for carrying out the equality programme;
- make sure that there is full consultation on policy and the action plan, and a means of reviewing progress and discussing solutions to problems.

└──

CHAPTER 3
Statistical Monitoring

Statistical monitoring is the key to any equal opportunity programme. It simply means comparing the employment patterns of men and women, of white staff and ethnic minority staff or of people with disabilities and others in your organisation, to identify any significant differences. You will need to look at their relative success rates in recruitment competitions; at the kinds of jobs they are doing; at the management levels they have reached; at relative promotion rates; and at relative resignation rates. A simple monitoring exercise will help you to assess how far your company is currently achieving equality of opportunity, identify areas where change is necessary, analyse and understand the causes of any inequality in your company, develop a strategy for change that makes the best use of available resources and measure the success of your equal opportunity programme.

The steps involved in a monitoring exercise are:

- collect and assemble your information and ensure that it is kept up to date;
- analyse your information;
- interpret the results of your analysis;
- identify where action is needed and what action is needed to achieve greater equality.

Collecting and assembling your information

Much of the information you need will be readily available in your organisation. Essentially it will consist of the kind of information regularly held on personnel records. For example:

age
educational qualifications

professional qualifications
previous work experience
length of employment with the company
type of job (e.g. clerical/typist/scientist/accountant/etc.)
grade/management level
section/department
staff appraisal or performance information/career development information.

You will also need to know for each member of staff or job applicant, their sex, ethnic origin and whether or not they have a disability.

Your company will almost certainly record the sex of the staff it employs on personnel records. Information about the sex of job applicants is also readily available from application forms. Information about the ethnic origins of staff or job applicants is, however, unlikely to be recorded and you cannot guess this from other available information (you cannot, for example, guess a person's ethnic origins from their nationality or place of birth). Instead, the information has to be collected.

You may already have some details about people in your organisation who are registered as disabled in order to comply with the Disabled Persons (Employment) Act 1944. This requires all employers who employ 20 people or more to keep records of their employment of people who are registered as disabled (see Chapter 9). However, this information is unlikely to be sufficient for effective monitoring of your company's equal opportunity policies.

Your first step in collecting and assembling monitoring information is, therefore, an exercise in obtaining information about ethnic origins and details of disability from staff and from job applicants.

Staff in post

There are two basic methods of collecting the data that you need for staff in post:

1. HEAD COUNT OR CENSUS BY MANAGEMENT

In this case, the responsibility for recording ethnic origins or disability information lies with local managers. Each manager is asked to record the ethnic origins of each member of staff for which he or she is responsible in discussion with the member of staff, or to record information about disability. Managers are given guidance on how to go about this. If necessary a manager will make his or her own assessment and inform the member of staff of the information that is being recorded.

2. SELF-COMPLETION QUESTIONNAIRE SURVEY

In this case a questionnaire is sent to all members of staff and it is the responsibility of each member of staff to record and return the information. An agreed classification of ethnic origin or disability is used and each member of staff allocates him or herself to one of the categories.

No one method is the right one: each has been used successfully. You should choose the method that is right for the size, nature and culture of your organisation. For example, self-completion questionnaires tend to work least well with a blue-collar workforce that has no tradition of form filling or the making of returns. Questionnaires are likely to be overlooked, disposed of and ignored, thus giving an unacceptably low response rate. In contrast, in a white collar organisation – especially one which is highly dispersed with regular routine returns to a region or centre – the completion of a questionnaire is not seen as unusual. Building societies are a good example of employers who have achieved over 95% replies to ethnic origin questionnaires.

You also need to choose the right method for the job you are doing. Collection from staff of information about their ethnic origin or disability, may need different approaches. There will be some cost advantage in collecting information about disability at the same time as you collect information about ethnic origin, but there is certainly no reason why both data collection exercises have to be done at the same time.

Each approach has advantages and disadvantages, some of which are listed below. You will need to consider these in the context of your own organisation and needs in order to decide which is the best method for you.

DATA COLLECTING METHODS

	Manager survey	Self-classification survey
Advantages	Quicker and cheaper to administer	Seen as more open
	Highest and most comprehensive returns	
	Makes managers responsible for success of survey	More acceptable – enables people to define themselves more clearly

Manager survey	Self-classification survey
In case of a disability survey, can encourage managers to get to know and understand the nature of the person's disability and quickly resolve any practical problems	Involves all staff directly in the exercise

	Manager survey	Self-classification survey
Disadvantages	Can be seen as less open	More costly and time consuming to administer
	Can be seen as less accurate in the case of ethnic origin information	Lower returns, which may have to be supplemented
	Managers may be reluctant to carry out the survey	

Which ever approach is adopted, however, it need not be a difficult or costly exercise and can have valuable spin-offs such as: providing an opportunity to explain what the company's equal opportunity policy is intended to achieve; winning support and commitment from staff for these policies; raising the profile or equal opportunity issues in your organisation; and obtaining information about any practical difficulties that staff with disabilities may be experiencing.

The key to successful data collection is its preparation and planning. Here is a summary of the decisions and steps you will need to take:

1. DECIDE ON WHICH METHOD YOU ARE GOING TO USE

If your company is unionised, discuss the survey with your *trade union representatives* and agree on the best approach – trade union support for a survey of this sort can help reassure staff of the value of the exercise. Also trade union officials can help provide information, encourage a high response rate and answer questions about the survey. Discuss the survey with a group of *staff with disabilities* or *ethnic minority* staff – involving staff with disabilities or black and Asian staff in the survey from the beginning can help give the exercise credibility, achieve support and help get the language and the style of a survey right.

2. TIMING

Decide on a date to carry out the survey, or head-count, with senior management and the trade unions, and allow plenty of time for preparation and briefing.

3. PILOT THE SURVEY FORM

Whether you are using a self-classification survey or a management headcount, you will need a standard form for making returns. This form should include: an explanation of the reason for the survey; a simple classification of ethnic origin or disability; a date of return; a contact point for queries and a contact point for returning the information. Whatever the survey, it always helps to try a questionnaire out on a few people before finalising it and sending it out; you may pick up points or language in the survey that are difficult to understand.

4. ARRANGE FOR THE SURVEY FORMS TO BE PRINTED

You will need to obtain copies of the survey forms well in advance. Those who will be responsible for briefing staff about the survey, for answering queries or for processing the forms when returned will need to be fully familiar with the forms before the survey begins.

5. BRIEF KEY STAFF ABOUT THE SURVEY

Whether you are using a self-classification survey or a management head-count, it is essential that line managers understand the purpose of the survey, because they will need to deal with queries and any concerns that staff may have.

Divide the workforce into enumeration units that are consistent with the smallest management teams. This will ensure that each member of staff will be briefed, and will reply to, or be counted by, someone with whom they are familiar and have regular contact.

6. PUBLICISE THE SURVEY

It is important to explain in any written questionnaire why the survey is being undertaken but it will also help to publicise the survey in advance, to let people know why and when the survey is being undertaken and how the information will be used. Routine company networks such as company newsletters and noticeboards can be used for this purpose. Promising to publicise the results will make people feel involved in the exercise and not just 'victims' of it.

Make sure the tone is firm and purposeful. In some organisations communications have been apologetic and nervous thereby reflecting senior management unease about ethnic monitoring. Adopting the right tone in communicating about the survey will help set a positive note for the survey or census itself whereas nervousness will filter down and be reflected in low response and poor co-operation.

Publicising the survey by way of a letter from the managing director or chair of the company, either in a staff newsletter or sent on an individual basis, will ensure that the exercise is seen to have the backing and interest of top management.

You should also set up a programme of cascading briefings. Make sure everyone is covered and arrange for feedback of any particular difficulties or objections that arise. If your company is unionised, you will find it particularly effective to carry out joint union and management briefings. Use outsiders to help with this briefing; they can tell staff about their own experiences of such surveys – it often reassures to know that anticipated difficulties did not arise.

7. ARRANGE A DATE AND SYSTEM FOR FOLLOW-UP OF NON-RETURNS

Whichever method you use, you will find that some people do not return the survey forms by the date required – in some cases this will simply be because people have forgotten; in others it will be because people are unwilling to provide the information. It is important to ensure that your data is as complete as it can be; a large non-response rate will undermine the validity of the data and will make reliable monitoring much more difficult. You will therefore need to set up an effective 'reminder' system.

One option is simply to send out a reminder note to all staff or – in the case of a management head count – to all managers. Another is to enter the data as received and at the follow-up date produce a printout of all those staff where the information is missing. A reminder letter can then be sent only to those people who have not replied.

8. SET UP A SYSTEM FOR DEALING WITH NON-RESPONDENTS AND ABSENTEES

Just as you need a reminder system to help achieve a full-response rate, you also need to plan for non-respondents. If your survey is by self-completion, make it clear from the start that managers will complete a return for non-respondents in consultation with them.

9. DECIDE HOW YOU ARE GOING TO HOLD THE DATA

For most organisations, the most sensible approach is to hold the information on computer. The numbers of staff you will be dealing with may be quite large and it will be quicker and easier to store the data, update it and analyse it using an appropriate computer software package. Many companies now produce standard software packages for storing and analysing personnel management information. (For more information, see 'Useful Addresses' p. 197.)

Whether the data is stored on computer records or on paper records, you must make sure that it is properly safeguarded. You must also make sure that your arrangements meet the requirements of the Data Protection Act 1984. This will involve ensuring that the data is checked with the individual before being entered into the personnel system, and that it is available to the individual for checking on request.

Access to name-linked data should be restricted to designated users. For most purposes, as in the examples below, what is needed is aggregated statistical data and there will be no need to identify individuals.

10. CHECK THE DATA

Before entering ethnic origin or disability data on to your personnel management information system, send a confidential note to every member of staff showing the information that will be entered on their record. Invite everyone to notify errors or amendments.

A similar check should be done at regular intervals when the data are in the system.

11. SET UP ARRANGEMENTS TO KEEP THE DATA UP TO DATE

You need to consider three aspects of keeping your data up to date. First you need to ensure that you obtain similar information for future staff who join the organisation – this is best achieved by using information collected on job application forms (see below).

Secondly, in the case of disability, you need to ensure that you obtain information about people who become disabled during their working career. This can be achieved by setting up a system whereby staff are sent a regular print-out (as above) of the personal details held on their personnel records with an invitation to correct or amend these.

Thirdly, you need to be able to keep track of people as they move through the organisation. This means that you will need to keep ethnic origin data or information about disabilities linked to a staff number or other unique identifier (such as payroll number).

Without these measures your survey will simply be a snapshot of the organisation at a particular point in time and will not allow you to use the data to monitor change.

12. MAKE SURE YOUR DATA ARE LINKED TO ALL THE OTHER PERSONNEL INFORMATION YOU WILL NEED

The main purpose of collecting ethnic origin, sex and disability information is to enable you to monitor employment patterns – promotions, resignations etc. You will therefore need to link your data to other information.

Key variables are: date of joining the organisation; date of appointment to current and previous job; grade, section or department in the organisation; type of job; age; educational/professional qualifications; marital status; absences on maternity leave or other special leave; staff appraisal/career development information – performance ratings and promotion ratings; training attended; working arrangements – part-time/jobshare/homeworking/full-time/etc.

13. PUBLICISE THE RESULTS

Once the data collection exercise has been completed and some initial analysis has been undertaken, publicise the results within the organisation. This will help keep a high profile for equal opportunity issues and help staff to feel involved and confident in the use of the information.

Providing managers with statistical summaries will help them to check progress in meeting equal opportunity objectives in their area of responsibility.

Statistical information for key indicators such as the representation of staff at different management levels or in different parts of the organisation should be made available to senior management and the trade unions to help them monitor progress in the organisation as a whole.

Collecting information on job applicants and new recruits

Collecting information about the ethnic origin, sex and disability of job applicants and new recruits is a vital part of any equal opportunity monitoring exercise; it is necessary in order to judge how good your recruitment and selections processes are. The information must be collected in a systematic way using the same categories of classification that you used in your staff in post survey.

It is now common practice for employers to ask for such information on application forms. Experience shows that you will obtain a much higher response rate if a question about ethnic origin or disability is simply included as part of the application form rather than as a separate insert. This approach will also make it easier to handle the information when the application form is received and avoids the possibility of the equal opportunities insert becoming lost.

Include questions about ethnic origin and disability in a separate section on the application form, along with other personal information such as sex, disability, marital status, age and address. Make clear that this information will be used for monitoring purposes to help your company measure its performance as an equal opportunity employer. The ethnic origin question can simply ask the applicant to indicate which of the ethnic origin categories listed applies to him or her (see page 49 for suggested classification).

A similar approach can be used for disability, but you should also make sure that sufficient space is allowed for any further information about the person's disability to be included that may be relevant to any special needs at the interview and that there is also room to include information about whether or not the applicant is registered as disabled. There should be three basic questions relating to disability, along the following lines:

1. Do you have any disability? Provide a classification of disabilities so that the applicant can indicate the kind of disability (see page 48 for suggested classification).
2. Are you registered as disabled under the Disabled Persons Employment Act 1944? Leave space to indicate registration number.
3. Are there any practical steps arising from your disability that you would like to be taken account of in arranging an interview? – e.g. interview to be arranged at a particular time of day to make travelling easier; an interpreter to be present at the interview etc.

If some applicants do not provide information about their ethnic origin, or about whether or not they have a disability, you should check on this at the interview just as you would check any other information that was absent from the application form.

Key variables for monitoring recruitment are: source of information about the job (e.g. newspaper advertisement/radio/job-centre/word of mouth) – this will help you assess if your recruitment advertising strategy is right; educational/professional qualifications; age; sex; previous work experience; performance in any qualifying test or in any other sifting process and performance at interview against an agreed set of criteria (see Chapter 5).

Collecting information about people with disabilities

Information about disability will help you not only to monitor the effectiveness of your company's equal opportunity policies, but also to ensure that the right *practical* steps are taken to deal with any difficulties that the working environment presents for staff with disabilities. For monitoring purposes, whether you are collecting information from job applicants and new recruits or from staff already in post, you will simply need to know whether someone has a 'significant' disability in employment terms, the nature of the disability and whether the person is registered as disabled under the Disabled Person's (Employment) Act, 1944.

More detailed information will be needed to deal effectively with any special needs of particular members of staff. For staff in post, this is best obtained by interviews with individuals, either as a follow up to a self-classification survey or by a manager if the approach adopted is a management classification survey. In a self-classification survey, you can simply add an extra question inviting staff to identify any special needs or practical problems arising from their disability that they would like to discuss with a manager or personnel manager.

DEFINITION OF DISABILITY

Your first decision in drawing up a classification of disability for your survey is how you are going to define disability. The majority of people have some kind of disability – they may, for example, be shortsighted and need to wear spectacles or contact lenses; they may have an allergy and have to avoid eating certain kinds of food; they may have back problems and be unable to play certain sports; or they may have a minor speech impediment. In most cases these disabilities present no barriers to employment and no significant practical difficulties at work. In terms of monitoring as part of an equal opportunity programme you will not, therefore, wish to record all the staff in your organisation who need to wear spectacles. What you do need to do is identify those people with a visual impairment that – without the right equipment or modifications to the job – does or could result in practical difficulties at work.

The Disabled Persons (Employment) Act, 1944 provides a definition of disability as follows:

'someone who on account of injury, disease or congenital
deformity, is substantially handicapped in obtaining or keeping
employment, or in undertaking work on his or her own account,
of a kind which apart from that injury, disease or deformity, would
be suited to his or her age, experience and qualifications.'

A simplified version of this definition will provide a suitable definition for you to use in your staff survey.

CLASSIFICATION OF DISABILITY

You will also need to establish a classification of disabilities. This should be as simple as possible; do not adopt a medical classification. You are interested in the effects of the disability and not its cause. People who have a hearing difficulty, for example, face a communication problem if they are in an environment that relies on the spoken word, and it is this communication problem that is likely to present and be seen to present a barrier to employment. The cause of the hearing difficulty for employment purposes is largely immaterial.

To make the best use of your information, you should try and adopt a definition which is comparable with definitions used in other employment surveys. This will ensure that you are able to compare your performance in recruiting people with disabilities against the representation of people with disabilities in the workforce as a whole. A helpful starting point is the classification used in a survey undertaken for the Department of Employment about people with disabilities at work (Employment and Handicap; Patricia Prescott-Clarke, Social and Community Planning Research; 1990). This survey used a fairly detailed classification of disability as follows. The percentages show what proportion of respondents (with a disability) who were economically active had each kind of disability.

locomotion	40%
reaching and stretching	6%
dexterity	16%
seeing	14%
hearing	20%
continence	8%
communication	9%
behaviour	18%
intellectual functioning	19%
consciousness	4%
digestion	9%
disfigurement	7%.

The most common kinds of disability were mobility problems, hearing difficulties, intellectual functioning, behavioural problems, dexterity problems and visual impairment. For monitoring purposes a classification of such detail is unnecessary. A simpler classification, which takes account of the main kinds of disability identified in the survey, will meet the needs of simplicity and comparability. For example:

• *mobility* Includes wheelchair users, people who depend on

artificial limbs or walking aids or have disabling conditions
such as rheumatism, arthritis or multiple sclerosis.

- *dexterity/co-ordination problem* Includes people who have impaired dexterity due to loss, partial loss or injury to hands and arms.
- *visual impairment* Includes people who are blind, have fractional sight or are partially sighted.
- *hearing impairment* Includes people who are deaf, partially deaf or hard of hearing.
- *behavioural* Includes people with, for example, psychoneuroses or psychoses.
- *intellectual functioning* For example as a result of dyslexia, Downs syndrome, cerebral palsy etc.
- *other* Includes people with epilepsy, diseases of the heart or circulatory system, speech impediments etc.

Collecting ethnic origin information

You will also need to decide on a classification of ethnic origin. Do not confuse questions about self-identity with monitoring categories; if you ask staff to classify themselves, you will find that you have almost as many ethnic origin categories as you have staff. This is because in effect, people are indicating how they see themselves; this is a complex and ever-changing matter of group and personal identity. But we do not need to know how people see themselves for monitoring purposes; what is needed is data on those who are likely to suffer racial discrimination. In other words, we are classifying how people are seen. Racial discrimination arises because of white people's perceptions of ethnic minority people, not because of someone's actual racial origins. So keep your classification as simple as possible.

These are the categories recommended by the Commission for Racial Equality and used in the 1991 Census.

CLASSIFYING ETHNIC ORIGIN
White
Black – African
Black – Caribbean
Black – other
Indian
Pakistani
Bangladeshi
Chinese
Other (please describe)

Using this classification for the collection of ethnic origin data about your staff and potential recruits will ensure that you can obtain local or national benchmark information from published Census information against which to measure your performance (for example, you will know the availability of applicants of different ethnic origin with certain qualifications).

Before you start

The idea of collecting ethnic origin data can arouse strong feelings and until recently it was considered to be too sensitive for employers to contemplate. Concern can also surround the collection of information about disability. Such monitoring is now commonplace, but, if your company is collecting information for the first time, or if you have to convince your senior managers, you and the people who will be involved in briefing staff need to know what objections are likely and how to meet these. Here are some of the concerns you may meet.

Q. *Isn't keeping ethnic records or information about people with disabilities discriminatory?*
A. Merely taking a note or record of a person's ethnic origin or disability is neutral and cannot be described as less or more favourable treatment.

Q. *Isn't collecting and keeping ethnic records offensive?*
A. This objection usually links the process to apartheid in South Africa or to the Nazis' requirements for Jews to be identified by racial origin. Again, the mere taking of a note or record is neutral. The *purpose* of having the information is to monitor progress and improve the position of ethnic minority people. In South Africa or Nazi Germany, the record was kept in order to treat people less favourably and to deny them rights.

Q. *Isn't a person's disability a private matter?*
A. Employers have a responsibility to ensure that the working environment does not prevent people with disabilities from fulfilling their potential and that recruitment and career development procedures do not discriminate against people with disabilities in any way. To fulfil this responsibility, employers must have information about disability. The information is collected on a confidential basis and in this way the privacy of the individual is respected. A full explanation of the purpose of the survey will allay any fears.

Q. *Can't the information be misused?*
A. Any personal data is open to misuse. So, like all such data, it will

be stored securely, with access to name-linked data restricted to designated users and for specific monitoring purposes.

Q. *Won't collecting the information draw attention to differences and cause resentment where none exists?*
A. Everyone knows who is black and who is Asian; one of the main reasons for racial discrimination is because ethnic minorities are visibly different from the majority. Noting these differences cannot create them. Perhaps the data collection process will raise awareness of differences. But, if prepared and undertaken openly with effective communication there will be a positive and purposeful outcome.

Q. *Won't monitoring lead to positive discrimination?*
A. There is no reason to suppose that the existence of records will lead to positive discrimination – it would be unlawful anyway. The data will be used to measure changes over time and to check on the reasons for differences between groups. It is a process to help managers decide on action within a policy framework.

Q. *Won't ethnic minorities object to the collection of this data?*
A. It is true that people from ethnic minorities are more likely to be sceptical about ethnic monitoring. But, where a full explanation is given there is no evidence that greater numbers of people from ethnic minorities refuse to cooperate.

Analysing your information; building a company profile

Once you have established a proper database you can begin to build up your company profile. Building a picture of employment patterns in your company will help establish how far your company is offering equality of opportunity, provide a benchmark against which to measure further progress and identify where action is needed.

It will also be valuable information to use in persuading others in your organisation that an equal opportunity programme is needed. Here are some of the key facts you will need to collect:

- number and percentage of women/men/ethnic minorities/people with disabilities in each job category or occupational group, e.g. secretary/technician/computer programmer/personnel manager/sales person etc.;
- number and percentage of men/women/ethnic minorities/people with disabilities at each management/grade level;
- number and percentage of women/men/ethnic minorities/people with disabilities amongst new entrants, over say the last five years;

- resignation rates of men/women/ethnic minorities/people with disabilities over, say, the last five years;
- promotion rates of men/women/ethnic minorities/people with disabilities within different occupational groups over, say, the last five years.

Pie charts, graphs and histograms can help display the information in an accessible and informative fashion. Here are some examples of the kinds of patterns you are likely to find in your organisation.

I REPRESENTATION OF WOMEN AT EACH MANAGEMENT LEVEL IN THE ORGANISATION

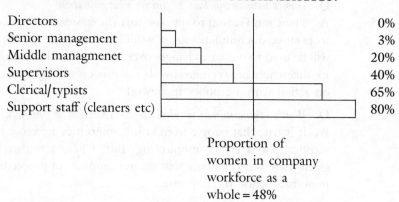

Directors	0%
Senior management	3%
Middle managmenet	20%
Supervisors	40%
Clerical/typists	65%
Support staff (cleaners etc)	80%

Proportion of women in company workforce as a whole = 48%

II TYPES OF JOBS DONE IN THE COMPANY BY PEOPLE WITH DISABILITIES

There are 1,500 staff with disabilities in the company of which

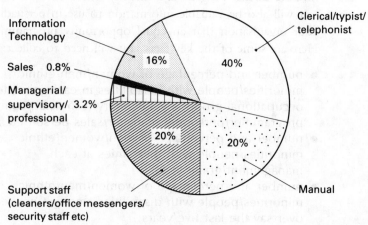

Information Technology

Sales 0.8%

Managerial/ supervisory/ professional 3.2%

Support staff (cleaners/office messengers/ security staff etc)

16%

40% Clerical/typist/ telephonist

20%

20% Manual

MAKING EQUAL OPPORTUNITIES WORK

There are 30,000 staff in the company altogether of which:

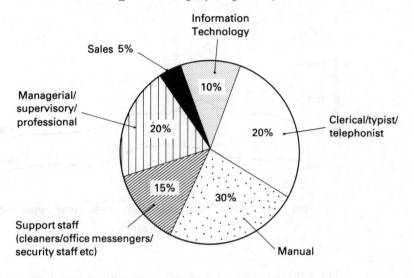

III RECRUITMENT OF ETHNIC MINORITIES

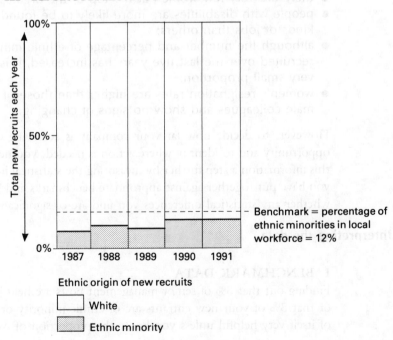

IV RESIGNATION RATES OF MEN AND WOMEN

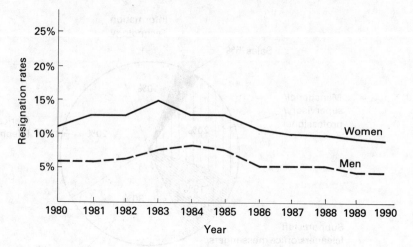

This kind of information provides you with an overall picture of where women/ethnic minorities/people with disabilities are in your organisation. The information you have obtained will already allow you to draw some conclusions. Looking at the information above, for example, we can see:

- there are very few women at the top of the organisation;
- people with disabilities are more likely to be found in some kinds of jobs than others;
- although the number and percentage of ethnic minorities recruited over the last five years has increased, it is still a very small proportion;
- women's resignation rates are higher than those of their male colleagues and show no signs of changing.

However, to decide how far your company is achieving equality of opportunity and to identify where action is needed, you need to take this information a step further by measuring the statistical information you have put together against appropriate benchmarks and by judging whether any statistical differences you find are of significance.

Interpreting the data

I BENCHMARK DATA

Finding out that 3% of senior management posts are held by women or that 3% of your new entrants are of ethnic minority origin is not of itself very helpful unless you know the proportion of women you might reasonably expect to find in senior management posts or the proportion of ethnic minorities you might reasonably expect to recruit. You need a benchmark against which to measure the 'performance' of your company.

In some cases, the benchmark may simply be the proportion of men or of white staff in similar positions – for example relative promotion rates of men or women or relative resignation rates. However, in other cases you may need a rather different kind of benchmark.

Recruitment

To interpret the new entrant figures, for example, you need to have some idea of the proportion of ethnic minorities or people with disabilities amongst the 'pool of potential recruits' (i.e. in the workforce as a whole). This will depend on where you are recruiting and the kind of job to which you are recruiting.

Nationally, about 5% of the workforce in 1990 were of ethnic minority origin. In London, this percentage was higher at 12%; in the West Midlands conurbation, the percentage was about 10%. Overall 70% of the economically active ethnic minority population lived in metropolitan county areas compared with 30% of whites. Among graduates, the percentage of ethnic minorities was about 8%. Similar information for women and for people with disabilities will also help you 'measure' your company's success in recruiting.

Here is a list of sources of statistical information that you can use for benchmark purposes:

- 1991 Census;
- Department of Employment Labour Force survey –
  published annually;
- Local authority sample surveys – many local authorities have
  undertaken their own surveys of the local working
  population; check to see if your own local authority has this
  kind of information available;
- UCCA: graduate destinations by gender published annually;
  some data on ethnic origin available from 1991;
- EOC annual publication – Women and Men in Britain
  Department of Employment – 1990 survey of 'Employment
  and Handicap.'

Career development

Similar kinds of benchmarks may be used to assess your company's performance in terms of the career development opportunities it offers. Relative promotion rates are obviously a key factor. Other ways of looking at career development opportunities are to compare the proportion of women/ethnic minorities/people with disabilities at different management levels with their representation in the company as a whole. In the above examples, women represented 48% of staff as a whole, but a much smaller proportion at middle and senior management levels. Similarly, less than 1% of staff with disabilities were working in sales whilst more than 50% were working either in clerical, typing, telephonist or general support jobs such as cleaners and office messengers.

You may also wish to look at your company's performance compared with the performance of other companies. Here again Department of Employment figures can help. You can obtain information about the proportion of women generally in management jobs or working as scientists etc. These kind of comparisons can be helpful in presenting a business case for your equal opportunity programme; if other companies are successfully recruiting ethnic minorities so should your company if it doesn't intend to miss out on some of the good people that your competitors may be recruiting.

II ASSESSING THE SIGNIFICANCE OF STATISTICAL DIFFERENCES

Complicated statistical analyses are unnecessary. You will need to do little more than calculate and compare percentages. But, you will need a basis for deciding whether any differences you find indicate inequality.

If, for example, we toss a coin 100 times and on 70 occasions the coin comes down 'heads', before using the coin again to make a choice between two options, we would want to know whether this 70% 'success rate' of 'heads' over 'tails' was pure chance or whether it indicated that the coin was weighted in favour of heads. Similarly, if you know that in 1990 the promotion rate of men in your organisation is 17% and the promotion rate of women was 10% we need to know whether this difference could simply have occurred by 'chance' or whether it indicates some bias in favour of men.

There are many different statistical tests of significance but the following approach is likely to be sufficient to enable you to identify potential bias or discrimination.

This approach is simply an estimate or 'rule of thumb'. It is called *the four-fifths rule* and has its origins in the US. The rule is contained in the Uniform Guidelines of Employee Selection Procedures. These were adopted in 1978 by four agencies in the US; the Equal Employment Opportunity Commission; the Civil Service Commission; the

Department of Labour and the Department of Justice. Courts in the USA have used the four-fifths rule as an indication of discriminatory practices. The four-fifth rule states that if the selection rate for any race, sex or ethnic origin is less than four-fifths or 80% of the rate of the group with the highest selection rate (e.g. white staff), this will be regarded as evidence of adverse impact (potential discrimination).

To take the above example of the promotion rates for men and women, we could use this rule to assess the significance of the statistical difference in success rates of men and women in the following way.

Example: Promotion rate for men $= 17\%$
          Promotion rate for women $= 10\%$

$$\frac{\text{Promotion rate for women}}{\text{Promotion rate for men}} = \frac{10\%}{17\%}$$

$$= \underline{58\%}$$

Conclusion: Women's promotion rates are only 58% of the promotion rates of men; this is less than the 'rule of thumb' of 80% or four-fifths and there is therefore evidence of potential bias or discrimination.

Identifying where action is needed

I MONITORING THE OUTCOMES OF DECISIONS MADE IN THE PERSONNEL PROCESS

Your company profile will help assess how far your organisation is currently achieving equality of opportunity and help you identify some of the areas where discrimination may be occurring.

Detailed monitoring of the outcomes of your company's personnel management practices will help you to analyse and understand how discrimination is occurring and also help you to develop an action plan and strategy for change.

Looking at the above example, we know that women have significantly lower promotion rates than men *but* we don't know why. There are a number of possible reasons:

- the eligibility criteria may sift out more women than men either because women are not getting the right kind of experience or because the criteria do not adequately take account of the working patterns and work history of women staff – long seniority requirements may, for example, militate against women, if your company has not in the past had many women workers;

- women may not choose to apply for promotion, perhaps because they are discouraged from doing so;
- those undertaking the selection board interview may be biased against women so that good women are failing to achieve promotion at the interview stage.

Different actions will be required for different problems. For example, you may need to look at the career development arrangements, adopt new or more appropriate sift criteria, ensure that in any publicity for promotion boards women are positively encouraged to apply, look at the way you select people to undertake promotion board interviewing and the training provided. Monitoring each stage of the promotion process will help you identify what is happening and what actions should be taken. Here is an example.

Monitoring a promotion board

	Women	Men
1. Number in the grade	100	450
2. Number meeting eligibility criteria – 3 years seniority	46	315
3. Proportion meeting eligibility criteria – i.e. 2 as % of 1	46%	70%
4. Number invited to interview	37	200
5. Proportion of eligible staff invited to interview – i.e. 4 as % of 3	80%	63%
6. Number of staff successful at interview	10	76
7. Proportion of staff invited to interview who were successful	27%	38%
8. Overall success rate of men and women – i.e. 6 as % of 1	10%	17%

ANALYSIS

Step 1

Is the overall success rate of women significantly different from that of men?

Yes – see above.

Step 2

At what stage in the promotion process is the difference in the success rate between men and women greatest?

At the eligibility criteria stage:

Men's success rate − women's success rate = 70% − 46% = 24%.

Step 3

Is this difference significant?

Apply four-fifths rule:

Women's success rate/men's success rate = 46/70 = 66%.

Yes − significant difference.

Step 4

Are there any significant differences at other stages of the promotion process?

Apply four-fifths rule to each stage of the process.

Selection for interview − line 5:

Men's success rate/woman's success rate = 63%/80% = 78%.

Significant difference.

Interview − line 7:

Women's success rate/men's success rate = 29/38 = 76%.

Significant difference.

INTERPRETATION

In the above example, we found that

- women have significantly lower promotion rates than men;
- that the biggest drop-out rate for women occurs at the eligibility criteria stage;
- of those men and women eligible for promotion a significantly smaller proportion of men than women are selected for interview on basis of performance and promotability markings;
- that a significantly smaller proportion of women than men are successful at the interview stage.

This suggests the following explanation. Firstly, the use of a three year seniority criterion in the above example clearly disadvantaged women with the result that a much smaller proportion of women than men were *considered* in the promotion process.

Secondly, it seems likely that at least some of the women who did not meet the three year seniority requirement would have met the standard set for judging performance or promotability. Those who had the necessary three years seniority were selected for interview on the basis of their performance markings and line manager assessment of

---

their promotability. More of the women that met the three year seniority requirement were selected for interview than men. This suggests that the effect of the seniority requirement was to sift out all but the very best women whilst sifting in a group of men with a much wider range of abilities. Whilst some men who may not, on the basis of their performance and promotability ratings, have been the most able candidates but may nevertheless have been good enough to be considered for and perhaps successfully in a promotion competition were sifted into the competition on the basis of seniority, the 'good enough' women appear to have been largely excluded from the chance to compete by the effect of the seniority requirement. Some of these women may well have been successful at interview if they had had the chance to compete along with men of similar abilities.

Thirdly, at interview women were less successful than men. Given the fact that, as we have said, the earlier section process appeared to exclude all but the very best women, it is surprising that women did less well than men at the interview stage. This may suggest bias on the part of the interview panel, inappropriate questioning or unfair selection criteria.

Action

First consider the eligibility requirement. Is three years seniority a necessary requirement of the grade above or is it simply used as a convenient, easy and long standing method of selection? What other eligibility options are there? Consider what qualities or experience really are necessary for the job.

Secondly, look at the criteria that were set by the interview panel in assessing suitability for the job, consider the questions that were asked and look at the remarks made by the interview panel for each candidate. Is there any evidence of discrimination (see Chapter 1, on 'Recognising Discrimination and Inequality'). Design and implement a new interview process, draw up a person-specification, set up a system for formally and systematically recording decisions made by the board and develop a training programme for board members. (For more information see Chapter 6.)

A similar approach can be used for monitoring the recruitment process. The same approach can also be applied to monitor access to training, staff appraisal information, job allocation, resignation rates. The flow chart in Figure 5 will give you some ideas on how to monitor ethnic origin in recruitment, what to look for and some examples of what actions to take (see Chapter 5 for further information).

IDENTIFYING WHERE ACTION IS NEEDED IN THE RECRUITMENT PROCESS

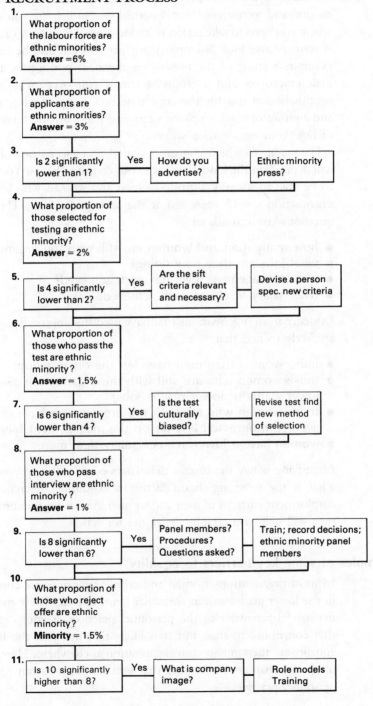

1. What proportion of the labour force are ethnic minorities? **Answer** = 6%

2. What proportion of applicants are ethnic minorities? **Answer** = 3%

3. Is 2 significantly lower than 1? — Yes — How do you advertise? — Ethnic minority press?

4. What proportion of those selected for testing are ethnic minority? **Answer** = 2%

5. Is 4 significantly lower than 2? — Yes — Are the sift criteria relevant and necessary? — Devise a person spec. new criteria

6. What proportion of those who pass the test are ethnic minority? **Answer** = 1.5%

7. Is 6 significantly lower than 4? — Yes — Is the test culturally biased? — Revise test find new method of selection

8. What proportion of those who pass interview are ethnic minority? **Answer** = 1%

9. Is 8 significantly lower than 6? — Yes — Panel members? Procedures? Questions asked? — Train; record decisions; ethnic minority panel members

10. What proportion of those who reject offer are ethnic minority? **Minority** = 1.5%

11. Is 10 significantly higher than 8? — Yes — What is company image? — Role models Training

II COHORT STUDIES

Producing a company profile and analysing current patterns of promotion and recruitment is an essential step in helping you to identify where you need to take action to tackle inequality in your organisation. A retrospective look at employment patterns can also be helpful. For example, a study of the present employment position of a group of male employees and a group of female employees who joined the organisation at roughly the same time or a group of white employees and a group of black employees can give you a broader understanding of how your organisation works.

The extent to which you can undertake a cohort study of this kind will depend on the kind of records your company keeps. You will need to be able to identify a group of men and women who joined your organisation say 15 years ago at the same grade level. The kinds of questions you can ask are:

- how many men and women are still with the organisation?
- what jobs are they now doing?
- what management level has each achieved?
- what salary level has each achieved?

Evidence from organisations that have used this approach suggests you are likely to find that:

- more women than men have left the organisation;
- those women who are still with the organisation are in lower status or lower profile jobs;
- those women who are with the organisation have on average progressed less far up the management hierarchy;
- women have a lower average salary than men.

Identifying where the biggest differences occur will help you establish what is the most significant factor in explaining differences in the employment patterns of men and women in your organisation. This in turn will help you establish priorities for action.

Examples of some key barriers to equality

In most organisations women and ethnic minorities are concentrated in the lower grades and in particular kinds of jobs. There may be particular characteristics of the personnel practices in your organisation that contribute to this. But it is likely that many of the barriers to equality are the same in your organisation as elsewhere. Here are some of the key barriers to equality that you should look out for in your personnel practices.

Information from the industrial tribunals, research and the general experiences of other employers point to the following kinds of practices that can lead to inequalities. They are discussed in more detail in subsequent chapters.

- inappropriate or unnecessary educational qualifications required;
- British and not foreign educational qualifications required;
- maximum age limits in recruitment;
- mobility requirements;
- seniority requirements
- selection tests;
- height or weight requirements.

CHECKLIST

- use an appropriate method of data collection;
- use the information gathered to judge how far your organisation is currently achieving equality of opportunity, to understand where discrimination is occurring and why, and to identify what actions are needed to prevent this;
- build a company profile to provide a snapshot of the position of women, ethnic minorities and people with disabilities in your organisation;
- look at the outcome of decisions made within your organisation about recruitment, promotion, training or job allocation
  - what to look for
    - under/over representation of one group
    - disproportionate success/rejection rate
  - how to evaluate
    - relate to appropriate benchmarks
    - compare differences using the four-fifths rule
  - then what?
    - establish causes
    - identify barriers
    - identify and check effectiveness of remedy.

CHAPTER 4
Image Building

Equal opportunity programmes make little difference to an organisation if you cannot persuade women, black people and people with disabilities to apply for jobs. Some companies have done a lot of work to break down the barriers which discourage applicants, and this chapter draws on their experience.

What are the barriers to applicants?

People build up a picture of an organisation from a variety of sources: from friends and family; from press, radio and television; from your recruitment literature and brochures, and advertising material; and from direct experience from your receptionists or telephonists, from your sales or delivery staff, or from your recruitment staff. The most common explanation for failure to change the make-up of an organisation is that 'they don't apply'. If you hear this said: check whether it is in fact so. Often, managers claim that women or ethnic minorities do not apply, but the real explanation is that they are screened out by the selection process. (See, further, Chapter 5.)

Discovering the reasons for low application rates

Some large organisations have carried out research surveys to find out why women, people with disabilities, or black and Asian people do not apply for jobs. Surveys of this kind are expensive, and are necessary only for very large employers or for an entire industry.

For example, the civil service commissioned the following survey: Cabinet Office (Management and Personnel Office) 'Survey of School Leaver Attitudes to Work in the Civil Service' (SCPR 1986). This found that both white and ethnic minority school leavers thought that the civil service was a white, middle-class, male organisation. Black and Asian young people and white females also believed that they would not progress; because women and ethnic minorities were confined to lower-level jobs. Asian young people were not attracted because they could not identify a defined career or job.

This information was used for local advertising campaigns aimed at dispelling these perceptions; for example defining careers in administration; or giving case histories of successful women and ethnic minorities; school liaison officers were appointed, including as many young women and ethnic minority civil servants as possible.

Similarly, in 1988 the 'Construction Industry Training Board Survey' found that young women and ethnic minorities saw the industry as not for them. Women 'generally felt that they would not be treated as equals in the construction industry; and there was little chance of getting in. Even if they did, they would not get a good job, and would face sexual harassment.'

Feedback from applicants

Useful information about how your company is seen can be obtained from contact with applicants or potential applicants.

For example, the Association of Graduate Recruiters (AGR) and Association of Graduate Careers Advisory Services (AGCAS) held seminars with university and polytechnic final year students to find out what influenced them, and particularly women, and black and Asian students in applying for opportunities. Factors mentioned were:

- recruitment literature and other promotional material;
- career break schemes;
- history of equal pay and employment of women;
- history of recruiting ethnic minorities into careers and management;
- personal contacts – friends who had got on;
- meeting women and ethnic minority recruitment staff;
- a professional qualification or career particularly appealed to Asian students;
- recruiters did not contact ethnic minority student societies.

Some companies had talked to school leavers, careers services or job centres, their own staff and to applicants for feedback. Factors mentioned by candidates or by careers services and job centre staff included:

- hostile or unwelcoming receptionist or 'gate' staff;
- a belief by women or ethnic minorities that the company was 'not for them'. Sometimes this was from the company reflecting an 'up-market' advertising image, or a 'traditional' or 'exclusive' image (interpreted as 'white male');

- negative images held by parents;
- publicity given to industrial tribunal cases, and in particular, a strong defensive posture by the company. This was seen as the company caring more about its reputation at the expense of black people and/or women. Publicity about cases leads to great scepticism about equal opportunity statements;
- 'coded' messages given by personnel staff are interpreted (sometimes wrongly) by applicants and careers or agency staff as 'no ethnic minorities' or 'no women' or 'no men'. Examples are

  must speak clear English or good speaking voice (='no ethnic minorities'),
  attractive personality (='a woman')
  heavy or outdoor work (='a man').

We have seen examples of barriers in search methods in Chapter 1.

Attracting applicants

How you need to target and attract under-represented groups to your company will depend on what has caused the under-representation. It is most likely that there will be several reasons. There are two main lessons which can be learned from experienced companies.

First, there is no instant solution. Changing perceptions which have built up over 10 or 15 years will take several years of sustained efforts. You have to invest time or resources for at least two years.

Secondly, personal contact is essential to build community networks. Once you have successfully recruited a significant proportion of ethnic minorities, women and people with disabilities, this will have a 'multiplier' effect and people from these groups will apply without special efforts being made to target them. The critical level varies; but for ethnic minorities it seems to be at least 10 to 15% of staff.

Image building

Here are some ways in which your company can promote a diverse image.

- Include positive images of white, black and Asian men and women in your promotional literature *and* in your advertising. Do not show them all in stereotypical roles or low-status job (e.g. male engineers; female secretaries; black cleaners).

  If you do not have black senior or white-collar staff

someone may object that such pictures give a false image of your company. Answer that this is a marketing campaign, designed to change perceptions. Argue that your product advertising presents a positive image of your brands.

- Ask your advertising staff to use minorities and women in non-traditional roles, especially if your company uses television and mass media.
- Make sure the literature is in non-sexist language – for example do not use the male pronoun for managers or traditionally male jobs.
- If you are appealing to school leavers, produce literature for parents, in their mother tongue for Asian communities (Gujerati, Hindi, Urdu, Punjabi, depending on your local market. In some localities you may need Chinese, Turkish or Greek).
- Advertise jobs and your product in the ethnic minority press, and in mass-circulation women's magazines. Although this may not produce many applicants, it is a powerful way of changing your image.
- Use local radio, e.g. reggae or Asian music stations, for advertising.
- Find good 'human-interest' case studies of female and ethnic minority success stories in your company. Ask the women's press or ethnic minority press to write up a feature. This has been done by the Department of the Environment and the National Westminster Bank and was a good way of letting potential applicants know about life on the 'inside'.
- Attend job fairs and careers fairs with young women and ethnic minority staff coming along to make sure first-hand, recent experience is available.

Links with education and careers services

Building direct links with school, university, polytechnic and further education careers services, and your local careers service ensures that all potential candidates receive information about your company. The link needed will, of course, vary according to the job, but can include the following.

- Talking to careers officers in schools with high numbers of ethnic minorities or in single sex schools. Offer to give seminars about non-traditional careers such as engineering for girls or for 'caring' jobs such as nursing for boys. Ask careers officers why they consider few ethnic minority men or women apply.

- Set up work experience, work shadowing or 'taster' schemes to give under-represented groups a chance to see the work for themselves. In 1990, BBC radio targeted ethnic minorities for their work placements, because these groups were not well represented in radio.
- Give presentations to sixth forms, or where career choices are made early (e.g. sciences versus arts) to third years.
- Make contact with colleges offering mature entry or access courses to people looking for a second career or returners. Give presentations and speak to careers officers.
- Run seminars/workshops with careers services, to give information about your company, for students, or school leavers or parents. You will get useful feedback about their perceptions. Where the parents speak little English, use interpreters.
- Arrange company/plant tours, targeting schools or careers services with links with under-represented groups, and girls' clubs or schools.
- Use 'adoption' sponsorship or fellowship schemes to attract women and ethnic minorities to careers or professional areas where they are under-represented. The Windsor Fellowship was set up to help ethnic minority under-graduates in particular, to develop links with leading employers in the public and private sector. It does so by arranging for companies to sponsor ethnic minority under-graduates or fellows in their final two years of study. Sponsorship includes two periods of work experience or project work with the sponsoring company during the summer vacation. The fellowship also arranges a personal development training programme and a community project for fellows. (See 'Useful addresses' section). WISE (Women Into Science and Engineering) was set up in 1984 by the Engineering Council and the EOC to encourage more women and girls into careers in science and engineering.
- Take part in COMPACT schemes which will link up local employers and schools. In these schemes, employers and final year pupils at a local secondary school reach agreement ('a compact') on improved punctuality, attendance and exam results, and work experience, and if targets are met, a job guarantee. Other similar partnership schemes have been developed with the help of Task Forces, for example, the North Peckham Task Force, the BBC and a training organisation (Fullemploy) set up office skills training for local people, most of whom were ethnic minorities. The success of these schemes lies in the involvement of

employers, who ensure that any training is relevant to their requirements. Your local Training and Enterprise Council or Employment Service can supply details.
- Give presentations to ethnic minority student societies, or invite them to your open days/factory visits or other promotional events.
- Make sure your vacancy notices are displayed in inner city job centres and are not removed after the first few applicants have been rejected.

Community links

Creating face-to-face contact with ethnic minority communities, and community organisations and leaders can be a very good way of creating networks and breaking down barriers. Which organisation you need to contact will depend on your locality. For example, start with your local Racial Equality Councils (REC – formerly community relations councils). They will have a large local membership and will arrange for you to meet representatives from various local communities, to discuss what you want to do and how to do it.

In carrying out staff and applicant ethnic origin surveys, civil servants and a representative of civil service unions, gave a presentation at the local REC offices on what was being done and why. They also talked about how best to target ethnic minority recruits. They learned that a major barrier was the selection process, as everyone knew someone who had applied to a civil service department in the locality, and had been rejected, often because of failure at the qualifying test. Also, ask the advice of the REC on ways of contacting local black churches, mosques, temples and community groups.

It is also a good idea to sponsor local community events, e.g. a hockey tournament with Asian teams, musical events or a 'drop in' centre. Contact girls' clubs, women's community advice centres, law centres, welfare centres and voluntary organisations to discuss whether they can offer advice or help, together with organisations for people with disabilities, and take their advice on attracting applicants and on access.

In recruiting at high levels, look for professional ethnic minority organisations (e.g. the Society of Black Lawyers) and women's groups (e.g. Women in Banking, European Network of Women in Training). Find out about these from the REC, or from the local polytechnic/ university students' union or from the professional body itself.

Involve your advertising and promotions staff: do they invite ethnic minority organisations to promotional events?

Role models

Successful women and ethnic minority staff can make important role models, but especially if they are few in number, there may be problems if they are made to feel they are being used as a 'token'. And, in one case a professional Asian woman agreed to a pen-picture of her being used in a careers advertisement. After publication she received an abusive letter. Managers must give support to staff being used as role models and must take an opportunity for debriefing. Care must be taken that role models are not over-exposed or isolated.

Serving customers or clients in a diverse labour market

Many people will have direct contact with your organisations as a customer or client. Their experiences will affect their perceptions of your organisation, and in turn, this will influence under-represented groups. We have already referred to the need for all promotional material to reflect a diverse community. It is also important to consider your services. Ask yourself the following questions.

- Are they accessible to all groups
- Are they sensitive to, or do they meet the needs of ethnic minority customers or women?
- Is there an assumption that your customers are men (e.g. in do-it-yourself or hardware, or in motor vehicle sales or repair), or women or, worse, 'housewives' (e.g. in food retailing or domestic housewares), or white (in many service industries) or able-bodied (e.g. in department stores)?

How to offer services to a diverse community

It is not the purpose of this book to set out a list of customer care and market research principles. But here are some questions to put to your colleagues.

1. Does your market research look at different customer preferences for men and women; white and ethnic minority; and people with disabilities? Do products reflect these preferences? If not, these customers will go elsewhere.
2. Does customer service training include awareness of cultural diversity and how to avoid stereotyping? For example, a bank received unfavourable publicity because a white customer saw a notice advising counter staff to check all Nigerian customers. It was done because a couple of Nigerian people had been suspected of

chequebook fraud. But no one could explain how the staff would identify potential Nigerian fraudsters, other than by using their colour or race; as their names and addresses were not given. Many black customers could thus have been treated less favourably on racial grounds. Consider whether the bank would have advised their staff to check all Welsh customers because someone with a Welsh name and Cardiff address had been fraudulent! Sales training needs to alert staff to the dangers of making sexist or racist assumptions, and using stereotypes. If this is not done, you will lose customers.

3. Do sales staff and customer service staff reflect the diversity of the market? There are many examples of companies who have gained customers after appointing ethnic minorities. Littlewoods stores reported that many years ago they saw very few black customers in their Liverpool stores, but this changed when they appointed black sales staff. A building society reports that they gained two large accounts from local Asian businesses after appointing an Asian as a deputy branch manager.

WOMEN IN CONSTRUCTION ADVISORY GROUP

Extract from *Recruiting and employing women, a guide for construction employers.*

Checklist on recruiting women

- Tell the careers service, CITB area office, skillcentres and local jobcentres that you want to train and employ women. If they don't send anyone, keep on at them until they get the message. Spread the word locally.
- Make contact with local girls' schools. Ask to speak separately to the girls in mixed schools. Try to talk to them before they drop important subjects, as well as before they leave school. Talk to parent/teacher associations and school governors too.
- Contact organisations in your area like girls' clubs, training workshops and women's employment projects. Usually your local authority will be funding them and can tell you who to contact.
- Establish a number of adult traineeships for women. Often they can come from skillcentres or training workshops to complete their training with you. Some local authorities are offering grants to employers who take women on for training in traditionally male jobs. If your council doesn't do this why not get together with other employers to lobby them? After all your plans will benefit the whole community.

- What about your existing workforce? You may already be employing women, perhaps as clerical workers, who have got interested in the work you do and would like to train as craftswomen or technicians. Give them the chance to train.
- Advertise vacancies and traineeships where women as well as men will see them. The ethnic minority press and local papers are a good bet. The display pages will get you better results than small ads under a 'building jobs vacant' heading which may be overlooked by women unless you specifically welcome them to apply.
- Whether or not you can afford to use the display pages, always include a statement which welcomes women and people from ethnic minorities to apply. It is not illegal to say 'applications from women and people from ethnic minorities will be particularly welcomed'.
- If you use any recruitment literature, make sure it includes pictures of women doing construction jobs.
- Encourage any employer associations of which you are a member to improve the image of the industry, e.g. sponsoring competitions in local schools for essays or projects on women in the building industry.

Equal Opportunities Review, March/April 1990

CASE STUDY

How Leyland Daf built up a relationship with the Cherrywood Centre, a school for young people, many Asian, who are new to the country.

Though Leyland Daf's factory is in Washwood Heath, an area of Birmingham with large numbers of Asian residents, few of the local Asian young people were applying for training with them. The objective of the company was to attract applications from young people, particularly local Asians, who would not normally be aware of the training opportunities offered by Leyland Daf.

Staff from Leyland Daf's training department visited all schools in the area to discuss ways of setting up links. Encouraged by the success of these initial contacts, they decided to take the initiative further by developing special links with a particular school, the Cherrywood Centre, unique in having almost exclusively Asian pupils newly arrived in the UK.

After making contact with the centre, they attended a number of preliminary meetings there with staff, governors and parents. Representatives from two other firms involved with Ten Company Group initiatives – TSB and the BT subsidiary, Fulcrum Communications – were also present. These meetings went well, with staff and governors of the centre acting as interpreters where necessary. The result was an action plan. First, teachers, parents and community leaders and then young people from the centre, would visit Leyland Daf. Then, when everyone was familiar with the factory, Leyland Daf managers would go into the centre to talk about the training on offer.

The plan was successful. Parents and teachers saw Leyland Daf training at first hand. The young people met existing trainees; including young Asians, and learned about their experiences. By the time the Leyland Daf managers visited the centre to talk about their training, the young people knew enough about the company to be receptive. This initiative was followed by more visits between the company and the school, with some young people having work experience in the factory. Leyland Daf are continuing to strengthen their links with the Cherrywood Centre which has taken on special significance for the company through helping them broaden their understanding of the local Asian community.

Many of the Cherrywood young people and their parents speak little English, but by visiting Leyland Daf and seeing their training at first hand, they gained much greater awareness of the opportunities available than would have otherwise been possible. Leyland Daf have been conscious of moving into new territory through their links with the centre and have found the experience highly enriching. They have found that the potential of young Asians can often be masked by their lack of English.

Lessons to be learned from this experience are that developing new relationships takes time – it is unrealistic to expect overnight success, and that showing young people and their parents your training and working environment is a valuable way of cementing relationships; teachers and parents often have good ideas to offer – listen to what they say and be prepared to act on their advice.

From: 'Working Together': produced for the Ten and Extended Companies Group by Cambridge Training and Development Ltd 1990.

MAKING EQUAL OPPORTUNITIES WORK

┌─ **CHECKLIST** ──────────────────────────────────────

- find out why few women, or applicants from the ethnic minorities apply to your company – is it because of your image or your recruitment advertising?
- target your recruitment efforts to change your company image
  - include positive images in recruitment literature and in product advertising
  - use young women and ethnic minority people in recruitment (e.g. job fairs)
  - use different advertising outlets; e.g. local radio; ethnic minority or womens' press;
- make links with specialised agencies, careers officers and schools;
- develop personal links and networks with your local communities and sponsor events;
- check the image presented in your customer services.

└──

CHAPTER 5
Recruitment and Selection

Many studies have shown that at each stage of the recruitment and selection process there is scope for racial or sex discrimination, and for discrimination against people with disabilities. Selection is highly affected by personal value systems. Interviews in particular can be the least reliable of all selection methods, yet they are universally used. Interviews are influenced by subtle differences in behaviour; and comunication barriers and discriminatory questions are common. At other stages, too, subjective decision-making is common, with feelings and assumptions, and not objective facts, influencing the outcome. What this amounts to is that organisations tend to reproduce themselves, because individual managers pick people like themselves. The higher up you look in an organisation, the more that personal qualities count in selection; and this increases the scope for subjectivity. In these circumstances, it is hardly surprising that white males predominate at senior levels, even in professions such as teaching, where the majority of staff are women.

It is not our purpose in this chapter to write a selection manual, but to concentrate on how to overcome the main barriers to selection which exclude women, people from ethnic minorities and people with disabilities. If you follow these suggestions, you will raise your standards and have more effective selection decisions, because this chapter is about objective selection and ways of recognising potential in all people.

Barriers to equality in selection

Barriers arise either because of the processes and requirements used in selection or in decision-making. They include the following.

Sifting or screening criteria

Arbitrary and biased criteria are often used simply to cut down the numbers of candidates. Examples include age limits ('under 35 preferred'); seniority fields (must have three years in the grade or five years' post-qualification); residential/location requirements ('must live within 25 miles of the site'); family circumstances ('prefer married people with a mortgage'); employment status (excluding part-time and unemployed applicants).

WHY ARE THESE CRITERIA UNFAIR?

The criteria are not irrelevant or unreasonable; but they are short-cuts and based on assumptions. Setting age limits is based on the assumption that older candidates cannot adapt or fit in; using fixed periods of experience is based on the assumption that less experienced candidates will not cope with the demands of a job. Location/residence requirements assume that people living elsewhere will arrive late; family and employment status requirements assume that married people are more stable and that unemployed people will lack the 'work ethic' and up-to-date work-related skills. All these assumptions will be false for very many candidates and their use will screen out large sections of the labour market. Because of under-achievement and late starts and (in the case of residence restrictions, because of the concentration of ethnic minorities in particular city sectors), their use will exclude more women, ethnic minorities and people with disabilities than white males and for full-time working will exclude women with dependents (and some men).

Qualifications and experience

This includes requirements for particular educational standards and for particular training or work experience.

It is common for employers to ask for 'five GCSEs' or 'three good "A" levels' or other educational criteria. Preference is given to candidates with good grades; or who gained their qualifications at one sitting; or to favoured educational institutions such as Oxford, Cambridge or Bristol universities. Employers frequently look for particular training, or a specific kind of management (such as commercial experience), or experience in the same industry.

There are many examples of employers who ask for educational qualifications or particular experience which is not relevant to the requirements of the job, and which is therefore unreasonable or unjustifiable. If you cannot show a relationship between your selection criteria and the needs of the job itself you are vulnerable to complaints of indirect discrimination. (See definition in Chapter 1.)

Again, it is not our intention to argue that these requirements are always unreasonable or unnecessary. But, as with the examples given for sifting, above, they are short-cuts and based on assumptions. It is assumed that a general educational level indicates good reasoning ability, and that particular experience brings relevant knowledge and skills. Often this is true, but not always. Many candidates with the ability and skills to do the job will not have the qualifications and experience specified; they may have left school early; have been denied a chance to follow your favoured career path; and may have gained the skills which you need in other ways. Again, women, ethnic minority people and those with disabilities will have missed out on opportunities for gaining qualifications or for management technical/professional careers. So you need to have some other way of spotting evidence of their skills and potential.

CASE STUDIES

1. A hotel in Oxford advertised for bar staff with 3 GCSEs, including maths. The manager's justification was that he would attract brighter candidates, who would be better at adding up and dealing with cash. Plainly educational qualifications are not necessary to be able to do mental additions.

2. A civil engineering company advertised for a management job in a new development in the inner city, specifying that candidates must be able to show a progressive career as a civil engineer. This specification would reduce the numbers of women who are greatly under-represented in civil engineering. However, if the advertisement had specified the essential components of the job (such as project management, planning and supervision) more women would have come forward.

The interview and decision-making

The interview is used to obtain information, to assess personality and motivation, and to assess acceptability. There are many problems associated with interviews:

- interviewers fail to get the facts;
- interviewers misjudge facts;

- biases and stereotypes affect judgements;
- subtle behavioural differences affect judgements;
- interviewers' judgements are biased by one favourable or one negative factor;
- judgements are inconsistent and unsystematic.

These factors affect all candidates, but are more likely to occur, and occur more frequently, when interviewers are assessing candidates who are not like themselves or who do not have a standard track record.

Aptitude and other selection tests

Because tests have a scientific basis, it is often assumed that all such tests are a more objective way of selecting applicants. This is certainly true if a test is closely related to the job, that is, it replicates many of the problem-solving or physical demands of the work, so that performance on the test would be mirrored by performance on the job. But many tests are not job-related, for the same reasons as an educational qualification may not be job-related. That is, standardized tests of reasoning which require a particular level of problem-solving, analysis and use of language and comprehension of instructions may be very far from the practical day-to-day decisions required in many jobs. Generally speaking the more abstract and general the test, the less likely it is to relate to a specific job. Generalised ability tests are suitable for school and college or university level recruitment, where candidates are being selected on their potential, rather than for a particular job.

Another problem inherent in the use of selection tests is that, because they are designed and tried out on samples consisting of mainly one dominant group (usually white males), tests tend to replicate the characteristics of this group. All tests are likely to be less effective predictors of performance for women and ethnic minority candidates, unless they have been specifically designed and trialed on samples which include these people. Very few tests in use in the UK today have been designed in this way.

A further problem with tests, as in any other selection, is that performance is affected by expectations and confidence, which in turn is affected by earlier experiences. Those who have suffered discrimination and consequently have missed out on opportunities, will tend to do less well in competition with others. So a valid test (that is a test which measures the abilities needed to do well on a job) may still disproportionately exclude women or ethnic minority people. In that event, other selection routes must be considered.

How to avoid bias

Objective selection

Effective selection methods have to include the following elements, in order to reduce or overcome the barriers we have identified.

JOB ANALYSIS
This is to identify components of the job and rank these by frequency and necessity.

Examples of job components
Cashier: machine operation, planning and organisation of work, attention to detail, oral communication, numeracy.

Management trainee: problem analysis and fact finding, planning and organising, delegation, monitoring and control of standards and results, oral communication, written communication, chairing small meetings, negotiating, persuading.

SKILLS/ABILITIES ANALYSIS
This is to identify skills/abilities needed to carry out the job components. These become the selection criteria.

Examples of skills/abilities analyses
Cashier:
- has worked or can learn to work with routine training, an on-line till (type specified);
- can establish course of action needed to carry out work;
- sensitivity – can show understanding of how actions and words affect customer relations and perceptions;
- attention to detail – can carry out small-scale tasks (e.g. item recording) and make sure there are no mistakes;
- oral communication – can deal with customer requests and colleagues effectively and positively and can explain simple facts;
- numeracy – can do or be trained to do simple cash additions or subtractions to supplement electronic till.

Trainee manager:
- analysis and fact-finding – can relate and compare facts and data from different sources; identify issues and relationships and causes, and can secure relevant information;

- judgement – able to identify courses of action and make decisions based on logical assumptions and awareness of likely consequences and outcomes;
- planning and organising – able to identify key tasks for self and staff in order to secure a specific outcome, and allocate tasks and estimate time for these to be done;
- delegation, monitoring and control – can allocate tasks with clear outcome to staff and procedures for checking on progress and can take action to rectify problems or regulate processes;
- negotiating and persuading – can make allowances for personal feelings and adapt style and tone to get staff working towards agreed tasks;
- oral communication – can be clear and effective in explaining, persuading, with groups and one to one;
- initiative – able to seek out people, take action to start a process, influence events or produce new ideas;
- written communication – able to express ideas, arguments and facts logically and in clear, plain prose;
- chairing meetings – able to start discussion, explain purpose, control and regulate discussion, and bring to a conclusion and consensus.

These are given as hypothetical examples, to show how jobs can be analysed into specific tasks, and how to identify the skills needed to carry these out. Higher level jobs need more subjective personal qualities, such as initiative, but even these qualities can be broken down into specific tasks which can be identified and measured.

Do-it-yourself job analysis

A job analysis is the cornerstone of objective non-discriminatory selection. If you do not have the job analysis you can make a start on a do-it-yourself basis, by analysing what your staff do in their current job(s):

- list all the tasks they carry out;
- rank them by frequency and duration;
- list outputs, results or standards;
- against each task, list skills or experience needed as the examples on page 80 showed.

Once the job has been analysed, and the skills and abilities identified, use these criteria to systematically evaluate facts about what applicants have done which demonstrates that they have such skills. This will help make sure decisions are consistent, and reduce the scope for bias.

Shortlisting

Most companies use an application form to screen out obviously unsuitable people and reduce numbers to be interviewed. But the design of many application forms makes it very difficult to identify the tasks people have done, and their skills. This leaves scope for staff to make assumptions. For example, if a candidate has poor academic grades, it will be assumed that this indicates lower academic ability than someone with high grades. This may be a false assumption; the candidate with poor grades may have had to overcome poor teaching, disrupted schooling or an under-resourced inner city school. Make sure that your shortlisting screen allows you to identify abilities in people who have not followed a standard track, because these people will be those who are constantly overlooked; women, especially women returners, people from ethnic minorities and those with disabilities.

THE APPLICATION FORM

If you follow these key principles you reduce the scope for staff to make assumptions.

Put all personal data (age, marital status, ethnic origin) on one sheet. These factors are not relevant to shortlisting. Data for health checks or personnel records or pension schemes can be obtained when job offers are made. And delete questions about academic qualifications unless they are essential to the job. For example, a general academic level may be necessary for a traineeship, or for a vocational or professional post.

Questions about experience should relate to the tasks and skills needed for the job. Candidates should be sent the list of key tasks and skills, and asked to state what they have done in their current or past jobs which is relevant to this list.

Questions about social activities should relate to the job and candidates should be asked to state how their social activities have given them relevant skills – for example, women returners to the labour market can describe the planning and organisation carried out in homecare and childcare activities.

Do not screen out candidates who have poor handwriting, poor spelling or poor written English language, unless written English is necessary for the job. Even if it is necessary, make sure that the level you are using is appropriate. For example, if the work involved completing job cards and similar records in manufacturing; what you need is an employee who can copy phrases from a specification or requisition on to a work card; and record simple numerical values from reading a gauge or similar equipment. Writing descriptive accounts of hobbies or previous jobs in an application form is not the same use of language and will be irrelevant.

BIODATA

This involves the identification of biographical information about all current job holders which correlates most closely with those who are good performers. It lists a wide range of information, ranging from hobbies and interests, school history and examinations, office holding, family and personal circumstances, and even likes and dislikes. Candidates are asked to give tick-box answers to describe themselves. It is not easy to guess, because some factors which might be considered generally desirable give a negative correlation (for example, a retailer found that having GCSEs did not correlate with being a good salesperson).

Biodata sifts work only in large volume pre-screening. Although the system is objective, it has the capacity to reproduce the existing population. If your good sales staff are 30-year-old white males who like photography and have two 'A' levels, that is what you will get from biodata. The system could have a highly discriminatory impact. Do not use 'off-the-shelf' biodata questionnaires, they will only work for the organisation for which they were designed. Do not use biodata until you have checked the results for differences between men and women; white, black and Asian; and people with disabilities.

RATING THE APPLICATION FORM

In order to maintain consistency and avoid bias, use a standardised format to obtain facts, and a rating scale which is determined against your job and skills analysis. Score the information against the job outline and from what the candidates state has been their experience (inside or outside work) and qualifications or other achievements. Wherever possible, the application form should only exclude those who are obviously unqualified, using only the most critical requirements.

There are many examples of employers who do not use an application form screen, but who use availability, and exclude candidates on the basis of trainability or other practical work-related tests and job simulations (see page 87 below). This would be more expensive and could be too demanding on resources if you are dealing with volume recruitment.

Objective interviewing

In order to avoid the many pitfalls of the interview, you need to make sure that you do the following:

- make the interview part of a wider selection process;
- make interviews systematic and structured to obtain key facts about the candidate's past experience and behaviour;
- give the candidate the job profile and skills/abilities specification in advance, and tell him or her how the interview questions relate to this specification;
- ensure interviewers are trained in questioning techniques (see Chapter 7);
- ensure that questions and the interview are planned so that all elements are covered;
- ensure that interviewers use a systematic rating to evaluate facts obtained on candidates;
- ensure that more than one interviewer is involved.

There are two important pre-requisites to interviewing, which help reduce sex or race bias. First, interviews should be planned. Candidates should be put at their ease and told how the interview will be carried out and how the information supplied in it will be used. This is a necessary equal opportunities practice because ethnic minority candidates in particular, may be unsure of what is expected of them, and may be more anxious than a white candidate, who may be more familiar with subtle interview rules, and more sensitive to non-verbal signals. Similarly, women, re-entering the labour market, may be at a disadvantage, because of lack of recent experience at interviews.

The second step to take is to use systematic questioning to establish facts about candidates, not opinions. Ethnic minority people, and indeed anyone from a different cultural background, will vary in the degree to which they are prepared to discuss a hypothetical or abstract question, or the way in which they will generalise. Systematic interview techniques will help reduce these variations.

GOOD INTERVIEW TECHNIQUES

Applicants should be asked for facts, ask them what they have done, not what they would like to do. If you want to test an applicant's ability to 'think on his or her feet' and develop an argument or explain an idea clearly and logically, or persuasively, you can do this in the context of a work-related problem, so that you are not inadvertently testing knowledge. Ask follow up questions to clarify answers; or obtain more detail.

It is also important to:

- record the information given;

- be encouraging about positive achievements, and understanding about problems faced;
- pace the interview to control the discussion and steer it on to relevant information;
- ask open questions – see examples given below.

PLANNING THE INTERVIEW

The interview should follow this outline:

- decide in advance how each interviewer will cover each aspect, e.g. the greeting and preliminary educational/social achievements, aspects of past/current job(s);
- identify and draft out questions which relate to each aspect of behaviour to be covered;
- greet the candidate and introduce interviewers;
- explain the purpose of the interview, describe the interview plan and how it relates to the job and selection criteria (e.g. 'we will ask you about your past jobs and experience; levels of responsibility; results achieved and problems overcome, to assess what analytical work you have done and how you had to plan it');
- allow each candidate up to 30 to 40 minutes, as necessary.

Examples of interview questions

Interviewees should be asked to describe a *task*, the *action* they took and the *outcome*.

- *To discuss examples of action using initiative:*
  'What changes have you made in your job to make it easier or more effective?'
  Follow up: 'What did you do to put these into operation?'
  'Who did you have to persuade and how did you do it?'
  'What was the result?'
- *To discuss tasks needing analysis:*
  'What sources of information do you use in your present job?'
  Follow up: 'How do you use this to keep you aware of problems?' 'What was the most difficult decision you had to make in the past year?'
  Follow up: 'What alternatives did you consider?' 'What was the outcome?'

This type of questioning allows you to obtain facts about the context, what was done and the consequences. It avoids ambiguity, for example claims about group action, vague statements, feelings and hypothetical statements, all of which are unreliable and capable of misinterpretation.

INTERVIEW REVIEW

As with shortlisting, use a standard form to evaluate candidates against the criteria identified. On page 86 there is an example of an interview rating form that does this:

Interview review rating

	1–5 rating (5 = related to job) (1 = not related)
1. *Educational background* subjects most and least enjoyed and why Out of school/social/family activities, organisational achievements	
2. *Work background* Major duties and responsibilities Any changes in responsibility. Examples of decisions taken	
3. *Planning and organisation* Description of how planned last week Systems for following up matters delegated Recurring problems and what was done	

4. *Initiative*
Example of projects started, why, what was
    different
Examples of work done over and above
    own tasks and why	

You may decide to use a cut-off score to select or decide on a final short-list (e.g. all scores above 12); or you may decide to rank candidates according to scores and shortlist or select the top three. The method you choose will depend partly on the ratio of applicants to vacancies. Before you make the selection, check which method (top-down or cut-off) has the least disproportionate effect on under-represented groups and on women. There is some evidence that the scores of sub-groups tend to 'bunch' at the top and bottom of a scale, possibly because those who do well must be expectionally good, to have overcome earlier disadvantage.

DOES MY SHORTLISTING AND INTERVIEW RATING SYSTEM DISCRIMINATE?

Even if you follow the steps outlined, you should still do a spot-check test on your system to make sure that it works for everyone.

Find an example of an applicant or someone on the staff, who is a late achiever; for example a married woman returner who had no paid employment for the previous 10 years; or an ethnic minority candidate who had a poor start, disrupted schooling and is under-employed in a relatively menial job, such as the graduate who works as an administrative officer.

Test out your shortlisting and interview ratings on the person you have chosen, with his or her help if possible. Make sure your system is sensitive to out-of-work and domestic attainments, organisational and planning tasks (planning a family event or outing) and negotiating skills (getting children to bed, solving family disputes, solving community disputes).

Spotting potential

Ethnic minorities and women have more often than not been unable to fulfil their potential, because they have not had the same chances as their peers or because of discrimination. Questions about what they have done at work and their attainments may conceal this. It is also important to find out about what they have done outside the workplace or outside their specific job as we have already seen above.

Other methods of assessing competence and potential

JOB SIMULATIONS
Many applicants prefer to be given work samples to supplement or replace ability tests. This is particularly true for disabled and ethnic minority candidates, who are known from studies to suffer higher levels of anxiety about performing on tests. Jobs involving specialised skills may require applicants to be given training first. For these, a standard sample of training material is given to applicants, followed by a test designed to measure their learning of the material. These are known as 'trainability' tests. But they are more suitable for manual than white-collar jobs, because they are labour-intensive, and have to be done in a standard way.

IN-TRAY EXERCISES AND ASSESSMENT CENTRES
These are a form of job simulation more applicable to managerial and professional levels.

During in-tray exercises applicants have to deal with accumulated letters, memoranda and reports, and decide on priorities, delegation of tasks, writing of reports, memoranda and plan and organise the work.

These test initiative, planning ability, management, problem analysis and judgement, and sensitivity.

In problem analysis applicants are asked to deal with a particular work-related problem, for example an irate customer, a shop steward, a complaint of sexual harassment, or to sell a product or interview an applicant.

These test oral communication, interview skills, sensitivity, stress tolerance, listening and negotiating skills.

As with other types of assessment, these exercises must be:

● job related;
● objectively evaluated against consistent criteria;
● fair and accurate – don't disadvantage candidates outside the work who may lack first-hand knowledge and don't use language or tasks above the job level;
● assessed by trained evaluators;
● monitored for their validity (i.e. candidates who do well must do well in the job), and for any disparate impact (i.e. don't rely on overall measures, check the results of women and men; white, black and Asian; and people with disabilities against an overall result – see Chapter 3).

Bias-free tests

Many of the factors already described as necessary for objective selection apply to tests. You can use professional psychologists to design your tests or you may want to buy an 'off-the-shelf' test. How do you make sure that the test will not discriminate by screening out women or people from ethnic minorities? Ask your test producer the following questions:

● Is it based on an analysis of the components of the job? If not, reject it, unless it is a standardised test, to be used for assessing general ability, e.g. for traineeships for higher level jobs, or for graduates or college leavers.
● If it *is* a test of general abilities, check what it measures and how it was developed, against the needs of your training or job analysis.
● Is it reliable? What information is there to show that the test has a good record for the job concerned? Or is its reliability based on out-of-date information? If so, reject it.
● Does the test measure the skills or abilities needed for the job?
  Content: Should contain representative samples of the job, namely problems to solve, the tasks (such as typing and so on), or manual dexterity or use of verbal or tabular material,

hand-eye co-ordination, which would have to be carried out. Basic aptitudes tested must all be necessary to the same extent as in the test samples.

Level: The test must measure abilities at the same level as the job. This is particularly relevant for tests of reasoning ability, verbal or numerical skills. The language used in setting the problem must not require more complex use of reading or comprehension than the ability being tested in the problem. In other words, if you need to check whether an applicant can collect information and draw up timetables or schedules from it, make sure this is what is being tested and not the language skills needed to understand the complex question.

Testing the test

Tests must be tried out before their general use on samples which include men and women, and the different ethnic groups in your labour market. These samples must be similar (e.g. length of time on the job, level of job; or for new entrants, similar age and educational background).

Test trials must show that performance on the test correlates closely with job performance for all groups.

Results for each question should be checked to make sure that women or ethnic minorities do not under-perform. For example, it has been shown that girls perform worse in numerical reasoning tests with unfamiliar settings (e.g. working out averages using cricket scores or velocity using motor vehicle speeds). Similar studies have shown that ethnic minorities under-performed on problems using particular media which are more familiar to the white, middle-class test designers (e.g. tennis scores or court bookings), and in comprehension problems using text with an outdated, formal style.

If your test producer has not made such checks, reject the test. It will have an adverse impact in use.

How closely do test results match job performance?

There should be a close relationship between test scores and performance on the job itself. Statistical studies are needed for this, using samples of at least 50 people. This is known as validation. It can be done by testing people currently doing the job and relating the results to an evaluation of their current performance; or by testing new entrants (but not using the results) and over time, checking test results to see whether or not they relate to their performance. These studies should also be done on samples containing men and women, and ethnic minority people, and as with trials, they should be matched. (The relationship should be the 0.05 level of statistical significance, i.e. a probability of no more than 1 in 20 to have occurred by chance.)

If the tests show a poor match with performance, a poor match for black or Asian people, or for women, *then* do not rely on tests alone, but also use the other methods described above.

If you want to use tests on numbers that are too small to test for validity, statistical checks can be done on other jobs with similar tasks. But this does not reduce the need to check the results for bias.

How to use tests

ADMINISTERING TESTS

Make sure that all candidates have time to do test practices, that is, samples of a similar test. Studies have shown that this helps reduce differences in results, particularly for older candidates and ethnic minorities, because it helps offset the lack of recent test-taking experience and reduces anxiety.

Make sure everyone understands the rules, for example, whether to leave questions unfinished and whether and when to turn over pages. Don't assume that all candidates know this.

Make sure that enough time is given for the test. This will be particularly important for people with disabilities. Studies have also shown that older people and ethnic minorities are more likely to give up earlier, again because of unfamiliarity with tests. Don't let the real test be whether or not you can perform at speed, if such time limits are not needed for the job.

Ensure that test administrators are encouraging and helpful. Try to provide an opportunity for applicants to re-test, with different materials if needed.

USING TEST RESULTS

Raw scores are compared with a 'norm' supplied by the test designer, to make sure that the scores of your group are typical. For some jobs, separate norms will be given for different age groups, for men and women and ethnic minorities. Use them as guidance; if your results are very different, you need to be careful about using them; because your applicant pool is probably atypical, look at other assessment methods too. Selections can be based on a cut-off score (no one with less than the chosen score is selected) or on a ranking (top 10 are selected).

Check which method of scoring produces the least adverse impact; this will depend on the distribution of marks between different groups.

MONITORING RESULTS

In Chapter 3 we describe how to monitor the results of selection. If you find that men and women, white and black or Asian or people with disabilities perform less well, here are some solutions you can use, (depending on the reasons for the difference).

- Use another assessment method.
- Check the job analysis, is it still reliable or has the job changed?
- Is the assessment at the right level for the job and the applicants? If not you will need to use another method, or invest in post-recruitment training.
- Can the job or entry level be redesigned?
- Is your training deficient? Do assessors and interviewers need re-training? Personnel staff often grumble that however objective the selection process, managers in the end choose the people they want and ignore objective scores or find a reason for overriding them. If this occurs, you need to reconsider selection strategy: collect the evidence and make out a case for tighter manager accountability for meeting equality targets (see Chapter 2).
- Ethnic minority or women returners may need training to make up for skills or experience gaps (see Chapter 7).
- Does your recruitment drive need re-designing to attract qualified people from under-represented groups (see Chapter 4)?

- base selection on analysis of the essential tasks of the job and essential skills needed to carry these out;
- base decisions on assessment methods which use evidence of ability to carry out tasks which are similar to the tasks of the job;
- check all assessments to ensure they relate to job performance and are not over-emphasising qualities or skills which are not needed;
- monitor results by ethnic group, sex and disability to check for bias;
- make sure all staff involved in selection are trained and use a systematic process for their decisions;
- where you have an adverse impact consider the scope for training in the skills lacked by the group concerned.

CHAPTER 6
Promotion and Career Development

There are many barriers to promotion, which we will deal with in this chapter, in addition to defining core skills, or competencies. We look at appraisal systems and promotion panels, also accelerated development, or fast track programmes. Finally, we deal with encouraging under-represented groups.

Barriers to promotion

It is possible to show that equal opportunity programmes have had an effect on recruitment patterns which have resulted in increases in the numbers of women entering professions such as medicine and accountancy, and in lower level management. Similarly, ethnic minorities have slowly begun to be recruited into previously all-white jobs and professions. But there has been little such progress in senior management, even in professions such as teaching where women are the majority. This suggests that there may be additional barriers to those in recruitment which still have to be overcome. For example, research in a predominantly male industry showed that the lack of flexible working arrangements and career-break schemes was a deterrent to women (more on flexible working in Chapter 8). Hostility to or sexual bantering of women professionals was an additional pressure on women's careers. Women managers are judged by a male model, and if they are assertive they are viewed as 'too aggressive'. Women who work co-operatively rather than competitively are viewed as 'weak'. Women are also seen as unwilling to be mobile and unlikely to cope with stress or aggression, or less able to make headway in tough competitive circumstances.

Studies of the progress of white compared to ethnic minority people have also found that they have been denied promotion because of stereotypical judgements, especially to supervisory positions where they would manage white staff. Employers have openly admitted that the first member of an ethnic minority promoted to manager has to be twice as good as a white person because of fears of their 'unacceptability', or fears of a white backlash to any mistakes. There is evidence too that white managers consistently underrate the performance of ethnic minority staff, especially when assessing subjective qualities such as judgement, motivation and initiative, and inter-personal skills. The communication skills of ethnic minority staff are also more often found to be lacking and, finally, ethnic minority staff, like women, face the additional hurdle of being seen by white colleagues as 'not one of us'.

Managers may also fail to put forward women or ethnic minority staff in order to protect them. For example, a manager may feel that a woman should be shielded from aggressive competition in a male-only section or job; or an ethnic minority from a racist environment; or from having to be mobile, on the assumption that it would be too disruptive to a woman's domestic arrangements or too stressful for an Asian, say, to be away from his or her community. Similarly, a manager may not push forward a member of staff with a disability, again wishing to protect him or her from additional pressures.

The higher up one looks in an organisation, the more important become the subtle rules about corporate behaviour. Anyone who is seen as an outsider, and by definition this applies more to ethnic minority managers, will be overlooked. 'Not ready' and 'will not fit' are two common reasons for the failure of ethnic minorities to enter senior management.

These subtle rules and stereotypes underlie assessments in appraisal systems, where promotion and career development are tied together, so that opportunities are not open to competition and overall effects of procedures are never questioned. It is believed that white males are at the top, because they have succeeded on merit.

The 'glass ceiling'

The term the 'glass ceiling' is used to describe the level at which, in most organisations, women and ethnic minorities seem to cease to progress. Despite growing numbers of women and ethnic minorities entering career and management functions, few women and ethnic minorities are found at executive and senior decision-making levels.

Arguably it is too soon to expect significant numbers of ethnic minority senior managers and board members, given that they have relatively recently entered these occupations; but there is also little evidence that ethnic minorities have begun even to move into middle management in proportion to their numbers in lower levels. We can see some progress in the entry of women into middle management, but despite more than ten years of equal opportunity policies, as in the United States, few women reach very senior levels.

There are particular barriers at very senior levels. These include the way in which such positions are filled – informality, subjectivity and reliance on 'insider' networks are still common, and the way in which criteria for particular qualities and skills also tend to be subjective. Using influence – leadership and organisational power structures are ways in which senior managers reach top positions. The way in which promotion systems work – in many big organisations, promotion is from within, and few outsiders are recruited beyond junior management levels. Consequently – and also as women and ethnic minorities are more concentrated in lower skilled jobs and in more junior grades – there are not enough of them there to be promoted to top jobs.

Barriers to promotion can be summed up as follows:

- direct discrimination, e.g. preference for a male supervisor;
- stereotyped assessment criteria, e.g. assertiveness = management style;
- acceptability criteria, e.g. 'white male model', 'not one of us';
- higher standards applied, e.g. the first female or ethnic minority manager has to be better;
- inconsistent assessments, e.g. women rated highly on job performance but not on promotability criteria;
- requiring uniform career patterns, e.g. underrating time spent out of paid employment or age requirements;
- discriminatory systems, e.g. seniority fields, length of time in grade, unbroken service;
- 'closed' systems, e.g. vacancies not advertised and appointments made by line managers;
- hostile or demeaning work environment, e.g. sexual banter, racist jokes;
- inflexible working arrangements, e.g. long, unsocial hours;
- promotion interviews, e.g. arbitrary or hypothetical questions not related to practical skills needed.

All these factors can lead to the failure of women, ethnic minorities or people with disabilities to apply for promotion, and result in low expectations and under-developed potential.

Defining core skills and experience

The first step towards opening up promotion and career development to more women and ethnic minorities is to analyse jobs in order to identify the core skills and experience needed at each level. The same approach as has already been described in Chapter 5 is appropriate here. In this way, a hierarchy of essential competencies can be defined. These will form the basis of person specifications for each job, for assessment of performance and appraisal systems, and for career planning, staff training and development, and more widely, for succession planning.

Analysis of components of promotion system

If your managers or supervisors are predominantly white males, there is a likelihood that the analysis of the job and identification of core skills and competencies will reproduce the characteristics of the existing white, male job holders. This is particularly so when evaluating personal traits and other subjective management behaviour.

You can reduce this risk by taking the following steps.

- When analysing the key work tasks and outcomes, include samples from groups representing your workforce or labour market, women and men, white and ethnic minority people.
- Make sure you distinguish specific knowledge or skills which can be learned or acquired from those which are essential from the start.
- Make sure that the job analysis fully represents all the necessary tasks, that each is fully identified and ranked by frequency, duration and level of difficulty.
- Make sure that your assessment criteria measure (and if possible show a correlation with) the characteristics needed for successful job performance. As in recruitment, your assessment should be based on evidence of tasks performed rather than on hypothetical or subjective questions. This applies particularly to subjective qualities such as 'leadership' and 'judgement', which can be tested in specific problem-solving behaviour.
- Criteria for appraisal should also be used to identify career development and training needs.
- You should check and monitor the progress of men and women, white and ethnic minority staff, and people with disabilities. If there are differences in their rates of progress, look for the reasons, and feed the results into your job and skills analysis, and review assessment criteria (see Chapter 3).

Procedures

Openness and objectivity are vital to equality, to encourage people from under-represented groups to apply for promotion, training and advancement, and to allow all staff to consider their own career development, and have feedback on their performance. Make sure that you do the following.

- Advertise all suitable promotion or upward mobility opportunities.
- Where promotion is part of career development, make sure that all eligible candidates with the necessary experience or career needs are considered, not just the immediate pool or 'next in line'. For example, secretaries should be eligible to apply for entry to management training and for promotion to management.
- Avoid job restrictions on training opportunities (e.g. access dependent on grade or salary level). In particular, staff from under-represented groups should be encouraged to enter career development training.
- Use your key skills analysts (see above) to establish a career plan for all levels, to give opportunity for upward movement.
- Use your core skills analysis to establish a career plan for all levels, to give the opportunity for upward movement.
- Do not use departmental or divisional seniority systems to determine promotion. These almost invariably discriminate against women.
- Make sure the criteria for promotion and career development, and career plans are known to everyone, and that feedback is given to those who do not succeed, especially where training will be needed.
- Make sure managers encourage women to apply for non-traditional jobs and for professional or vocational training.

Performance appraisals

An objective, open and participative appraisal system can help increase opportunities for women, ethnic minorities and people with disabilities. It will make individuals' progress more systematic and structured. However, as with other assessment systems, you need to check that your managers' appraisals are not biased. Apply the following steps:

- performance ratings must be based on core skills;
- performance assessments must be based on analysis of tasks done, not on assumptions and inferences;

- assessment must be open and two-way – in other words done in discussion with your staff;
- checks must be built in, with a counter-signing officer and monitoring of outcomes. Any discriminatory patterns which arise must be discussed with your managers, and if necessary, the appraisal rating reviewed;
- managers must have had training in non-discriminatory assessment;
- managers should themselves have a specific equality objective, relating to their responsibility to encourage the development of their staff, and improve representation of target groups where they are concentrated in more junior levels.

Checking appraisals for inequality

Whether you are a counter-signing officer, or responsible for a team department or division, you have an important managerial role in checking for equality. There are several points to look out for. The first is subjective language used by men assessing women or whites assessing ethnic minority staff (see Chapter 1). For example, 'not ready for responsibility' may be a stereotyped judgement, be especially wary if job performance is good. Women and ethnic minorities have often been rated as good job performers, but not considered ready for promotion because of an unconscious expectation that white males are most suitable.

Next, look for inconsistency in self-assessment. Some women may be more open about their weaknesses and more self-critical; whereas some men may hide their failings. Managers should guard against assuming that these tendencies in fact that the male is better.

Also, look for inconsistent ratings between job performance and future potential (see above). It is common for an organisation to find discriminatory patterns in performance appraisal systems when they begin to monitor them. Examples include equal ratings or higher ratings with male colleagues for women on the more objective performance criteria such as work output or quality of work, but for them to be marked lower on subjective criteria such as initiative and motivation. If this occurs across more than five comparable cases, you may have unconscious bias or stereotyping. Review these ratings with the line manager and challenge his or her assessments.

Finally, inadequate task allocation may result in a lower job performance rating. One common complaint from ethnic minority staff is that they are allocated a narrower range of tasks, in particular they are not given jobs which involve dealing with the public, or sensitive or 'high-profile' jobs which require them to represent the company, or make decisions with minimum supervision. This will result in disadvantage when staff are considered for promotion. Make sure that in planning job allocation, career moves and postings, ethnic minority staff are not overlooked for premium tasks.

Promotion systems

In general the less open and unsystematic your promotion system, the more likely it is to disadvantage under-represented groups, and to replicate the characteristics of senior managers currently in post. Some of the benefits and disadvantages of the more commonly-used systems for equality of opportunity are dealt within the following pages. Please note that this is not an analysis of promotion systems as such; we are looking at equality. There may be other advantages to your company; you will have to weigh these against the equality effects.

Advantages and disadvantages of different promotion systems

Method	Advantages	Disadvantages
Assessment Centres	If task-based, therefore can be more objective.	Can be expensive and time consuming
	Can also identify training and development needs.	Can favour experience over potential.
	Candidates can be given preparatory training before entering assessment.	Little research on possible race or gender bias.
	Can introduce flexibility.	
Interviews	Can be quickest and cheapest method.	Least reliable and subject to interview bias.
Succession Planning	Can be made systematic and objective but see disadvantages.	Tends to be 'closed' and biased.
	Cheapest and easiest.	Difficult to monitor results and criteria.

(Continued)

Advantages and disadvantages of different promotion systems
(*continued*)

Method	Advantages	Disadvantages
Career planning/career development/appraisal system	If based on job task and role analysis, can be objective.	Expensive.
	If based on openness, can be perceived as fair and participative.	Requires training and development investment and back-up
	If systematic and linked to training, can be best for individual development.	
	Results can be monitored.	

Competitive promotion

In many organisations, especially in the public sector, promotion is competitive, with opportunities advertised internally, open to all applicants, although usually with an eligibility criteria such as experience in the grade below or a specialist qualification for professional posts. In local government, in order to attract people from under-represented categories into higher levels, promotion opportunities are advertised externally. Open competition for promotion can have two major advantages. First, it can speed the entry of women and ethnic minorities to higher level jobs, especially if it is part of an access training or positive action strategy (see Chapter 7). Secondly, it brings fresh ideas and diverse experience into the organisation, thereby enhancing flexibility and receptiveness to change.

However, competitive promotion does not guarantee that your organisation will change. If you apply narrow selection criteria, relying on stereotyped experience, you will find that the new entrants still tend to be white males. It is essential for competitive promotion systems to be introduced at the same time as you review your selection criteria (see Chapter 5).

Interviews, promotion panels and boards

If your company has open competition for promotion, there is likely to be a competitive interview at which short-listed candidates appear before a decision is made about their suitability. Chapter 5 sets out the steps to follow to reduce possible interview bias. Here are some other checks to help avoid bias.

- *Panel composition:* Interviews by two or more panel members, if possible including a woman or ethnic minority person, can help reduce individual bias.
- *Procedures:* Should be standardised with a systematic rating scale.
- *Training:* Interviewers should be trained so that they are aware of the ways in which bias can operate.
- *Monitoring:* The chair of interview panels should monitor ratings as interviews are carried out. This is to keep an eye out for disparities between men's and women's ratings, white and ethnic minorities, and of candidates with disabilities. If differences are occurring, the panel can review their assessments before any final decision is made.
- *Guidelines:* You should issue interviewing guidelines to all employees before they attend interviews. This should set out the criteria for promotion and explain how the interview will relate to these criteria.

Selection for promotion without interview

If promotion is decided on the basis of appraisal and career development plans, similar checks against bias should be built into the system. Ensure the following.

- The criteria for promotion should be known to all who are eligible, that is all those who have been rated favourably in appraisal systems or who have completed the necessary range of postings to achieve the relevant experience.
- All eligible staff should be rated systematically against these criteria, by two or more managers. The ratings should then be averaged to give an overall ranking of candidates.
- Decisions should be monitored to check whether there is consistent application of the criteria, and to check for disparities in rating and ranking between men and women, white and ethnic minorities, or lower rates for people with disabilities (see Chapter 3 for details on how to look for disparities). If differences exist, look again at the ratings of near-miss people. If the differences persist over time or across large numbers, and a skill or experience gap has emerged you should review career development and training arrangements, and make sure that people from under-represented groups particularly benefit, so as to close the gap.

- Managers involved in selection for promotion must have been trained in unbiased decision-making in a similar way to those carrying out recruitment and interviewing.

How to identify potential

Once again, you need to return to the job or grade for which training and development is being considered and analyse its component tasks. For example, if there is under-representation in management, the core skills needed may include:

- ability to analyse problems and identify appropriate solutions;
- ability to present ideas and arguments clearly and in appropriate style;
- ability to work with colleagues and subordinates and involve them;
- ability to define realistic outcomes and make plans for their achievement and identify resources;
- ability to identify own tasks and to take appropriate action and persuade others of the need for action to circumvent difficulties.

There will be other core skills such as the ability to persuade, take decisions quickly, work alone or under pressure, do oral presentations, which will vary according to the organisation and job. Rank skills according to their importance and frequency.

Analyse the education, experience and, in particular, specific projects carried out by under-represented groups. Identify achievements, including those occurring out of work which show evidence of the skills or abilities needed for progression. Use this to identify developmental needs. If necessary, carry out work simulations to assess competencies, such as those used in assessment centres. You now have the components for an accelerated career development programme. Examples of fast-track programmes (remembering that such programmes can only be job and company specific) include:

- professional or technical skills training, such as financial management or data processing/analysis. If there are new areas of work requiring specific skills it may also be helpful for trainees to have short (three to five days) 'taster' attachments;
- role play and team tasks which give experience of dealing with crisis and managing in conflict;
- allocation to projects and task forces which give experience of problem-solving;

- allocation to front-line, sensitive or key work to give experience of representing the company;
- presentational skills training to improve oral communications and help improve self-confidence;
- support or mentoring arrangements, which may be provided by women's or black staff networks. The allocation to fast-track minorities and women of a personal mentor at two or three levels above, to give advice, counselling, support, and above all inside information on the informal rules and help build up contacts is also useful.

Fast-track staff development for under-represented groups

Many companies are familiar with special fast-track or accelerated development schemes for those considered to be 'high fliers', that is, staff with potential. Such schemes are often for graduate entrants. One way of speeding up the representation of women and ethnic minority staff into higher levels is to start a parallel accelerated development programme, aimed at people with potential from these groups. This is particularly important for companies with high numbers of these groups in lower level administrative and clerical jobs, and for 'blue-collar' organisations where the key problem is a failure to break through into first-line management.

Even if only some of the barriers listed above exist in your company, this still means that more women, ethnic minority staff and staff with disabilities will have under-achieved, compared with staff as a whole. If you also consider that these groups will have missed out on opportunities earlier in their jobs because of barriers in recruitment or in education, you have further indication of likely under-achievement. A fast-track development scheme would aim to make up for some of these missed opportunities, by targeting people with potential, and giving them practical help and experience through intensive training and career development, based on an analysis of their particular needs.

Encouraging under-represented groups

If your company has only white males working at senior levels, you have to take action to convince women and ethnic minorities that it is worth while for them to try to develop and advance themselves.

The fast-track career development scheme described above will give a positive message about your intentions, especially when participants start to gain promotion. But what else can be done to change aspirations? Here are some examples:

- talk to women and ethnic minority staff about their career hopes and frustrations, and feed this into your plans for training and development;

- talk to managers about why their staff apply or seek promotion (How are they encouraged? What more can be done?);
- find examples (such as case studies or award winners) of role models, to use in company recruitment literature and especially in your internal news letters and staff bulletins;
- encourage women and ethnic minority staff to be involved in cross-company events (e.g. conferences and promotional campaigns);
- seek out and use consultants, external trainers and advertising agencies which have women and minority staff themselves;
- arrange self-development training to help under-represented groups clarify their personal career plans and develop self-confidence and assertion skills;
- never assume that a women or an ethnic minority member of staff is not interested in promotion or development.

To sum up, the barriers to higher level progress come from assessment methods and an increasing emphasis on acceptability. These can be tackled by making the promotion criteria more open and job-related. Procedures should facilitate progression, and be open and accessible to all and the results should be monitored. There must be an objective procedure for appraising job performance in order to give feedback to staff and to develop their careers.

You must identify women and ethnic minorities with potential and set up a structured training and development package to increase their success rates in promotion. You must develop a positive climate through promotional campaigns and communication, and by training, to encourage under-represented groups to apply for advancement.

CASE STUDY—*Blueline Metropolitan Buses*

Mr Singh was employed as a busman in the company's southern region for 9 years; during his last two years he was asked to work as an acting charge-hand for 14 months. His job was to supervise a team cleaning buses and coaches.

In July 1990, Mr Singh heard that the chargehand post was available as a permanent vacancy, and he was told by his foreman, Mr Wright, that he should apply and submit an application. He did so, and was given a day's notice of the interview. The interview was by a two-man panel; the foreman

---

MAKING EQUAL OPPORTUNITIES WORK

(Mr Wright) and the section manager, (Mr Mercer). Mr Singh said that he was not asked questions about his experience as an acting chargehand, and was questioned about his sickness record. Mr Singh complained of racial discrimination when he heard that the successful candidate was a white man whom he had supervised, with a shorter length of service than himself, and who had had a warning for poor attendance. Three of the candidates were of Asian origin, and one (the successful one) was white. All were male.

The general manager looked into Mr Singh's allegations and advised him that he had been unsuccessful because he failed to answer the interview questions satisfactorily. It was accepted that Mr Singh had longer service and a better attendance record than the successful candidate.

Of the southern region staff, 5% were of Afro-Caribbean origin and 2% were Asian. One-third are bus-women and two-thirds are bus-men. All the chargehands are white males.

Was the promotion procedure a barrier?
No women applied.
The job was not advertised; Mr Singh heard about it.
Candidates were given no information about the selection criteria before interview.
Candidates were not given feedback on the results.

Were the selection criteria job-related?
Selection was based on performance at interview. How is this relevant to assessing capacity to supervise a cleaning crew? What were the criteria? What skills and abilities were needed?
Experience was not effectively evaluated. The complainant had already carried out the functions for 14 months.

Why did no women apply?
Was information passed via a male grapevine?
Is a chargehand perceived as a 'male' role?
What training or encouragement could be given to women and ethnic minority staff?

What action should Blueline take to improve their promotion practices?

Advertise the vacancy with clear criteria. In the wording of the advertisement, encourage women and ethnic minority people to apply. List the selection criteria and give it to the applicants before the interview.

Analyse the tasks needed to perform the job and base selection on these essential skills and experience and train interviewers. Also, monitor applications and results and analyse the training needs of women and ethnic minority staff in the applicant pool, and consider a developmental training programme that will help reduce under-representation. Give unsuccessful candidates feedback on what they need to do to be promoted (e.g. widen their job experience).

EXAMPLE

Career development
'We are concerned that career paths within the Company should reflect the situation in the workplace, traditionally the preserve of adult males in continuous employment, but now undergoing rapid and radical changes. More women are working now, either with a break for child-rearing, or continuously. Women are better qualified and more interested in meaningful jobs with prospects, and this is also true of black and ethnic minority people and those with disability.

As a company, we recognise that many employees in these groups may be under-using their abilities and qualifications, and we are committed to identifying such employees and providing them with opportunities to develop their potential.'

Check that: development policies or promotion and transfer are con-tinually revised and updated; qualifications and criteria for promotion and transfer are justifiable (for example, promotion on the basis of length of service may be interpreted as unlawful indirect discrimi-nation, as women are less likely to qualify); policies make it quite clear that promotion and transfer are open to all suitably qualified and experienced personnel; regular appraisal and performance reviews are made, discussions on potential, career development, and training are held with all employees (oral or written feedback on such interviews is to be made available to employees on request) and a formal process to identify employees with promotion potential is developed.

Also check that analysis of the staffing situation is used:

- to identify career structures and development processes;
- to identify alternative entry points to career paths;
- to check the career development progress of women, black people and ethnic minority groups and people with disability
- to check the proportions of women, black people and members of ethnic minority groups holding management positions compared to lower zoned or graded jobs.

From: Littlewoods Organisation PLC.
Equal Opportunities Code of Practice.

CHECKLIST

- make sure your promotion systems and assessment criteria do not contain barriers to the progression of women and ethnic minorities;
- analyse the job and define core skills and experience as the basis of any assessment for promotion, career development and posting;
- make sure performance appraisal systems are open and are not biased against women and ethnic minority staff;
- train those involved in assessment and in promotion interviews;
- make promotion panels/boards operate systematically against pre-defined criteria;
- if women or ethnic minority people are under-represented at higher levels, analyse core skills and needs and identify people with potential for a fast-track development programme;
- encourage under-represented people to apply for a development scheme, or promotion and for key postings;
- monitor progression and use the results to decide on further positive action.

CHAPTER 7
Equal Opportunities Training

In this chapter we look at what training is, and why it should take place. We deal with the pitfalls of training, its three basic components and how to identify training needs. Further on we examine skills and competencies and training methods, finishing with evaluation and positive action training.

What is training for equal opportunities?

Training is for preparing people to make decisions and carry out tasks. Since equal opportunities programmes are designed to change practices and the make-up of an organisation, training is essential, and will be a key element contributing to effective change. How and what the training should be will vary according to the stage of an equal opportunity programme which your company has reached, and the function level and experience of staff to be trained.

Training is necessary for the following reasons:

- to raise awareness;
- to get things started or give a signal that things are moving;
- to get support;
- to develop a strategy for changes in practices;
- to impart information, knowledge and understanding;
- to give new skills and enhance experience;
- to make up for past under-achievement or lack of experience and develop confidence.

Your training programme must be built into the equal opportunities plan, and be part of the process of change. This means that training course content and objectives must be integral to the equal opportunities plan. For example, do not waste resources on training staff in non-discriminatory selection, if they have no authority to put into effect their new knowledge and skills, because the company/recruitment policy has not changed.

The pitfalls

What are the signs that your equal opportunities training is not effective?

UNPOPULARITY

Trainees will not wish to attend training which is seen as a way of changing their attitudes. Often this has been because too much emphasis is put on being judgemental; trainees have been made to feel uncomfortable or guilty, but have been given no help in dealing with such feelings. This results in their rejection of the training and resentment of equal opportunities.

IRRELEVANCE

Do participants have the authority to change practices as a result of the training? The training must be related to individual and organisational needs, and be pitched at the appropriate level. For example, a workshop on non-discriminatory recruitment and selection, with some excellent case studies, attended by managers whose only involvement in recruitment is in attracting applicants, and where selection was still handled centrally, using tests and interviews which are highly discriminatory, changes nothing and any positive feelings generated will be wasted.

INEFFECTIVENESS

Much equal opportunities training has been ineffective because it is too theoretical or generalised, often because a standard 'off-the-shelf' package is used, or because trainers are left to design the course and training methods, and they lack a clear remit. In these circumstances, the training tends to concentrate on the descriptive, such as an explanation of the law and Codes of Practice; it is too theoretical.

Pitfalls for trainers

Trainers are often unclear of their role and objectives, for example, were they being asked to challenge attitudes or behaviour? If the latter, how do they deal with racist or sexist comments? If they are changing behaviour, how do they deal with trainees who fail to respond to the training? What do they do about changing practices when neither they nor the trainees have the power to do anything? Trainers dislike sending trainees back without a clear remit to carry out what is necessary.

Trainers can also feel ill at ease with trainees' emotional reactions. Even where training concentrates on awareness and skills, trainees will, unlike any other management training, show an emotional reaction; some will become upset and angry at what they see as 'special treatment' or 'positive discrimination'. Others, for example, women and ethnic minorities, will become angry at what they see as sexist or racist attitudes, or unwillingness to face the issues. Such reactions must be expected; trainers need to know how to deal with them positively.

Trainers can often feel that they are not equipped with material which is relevant to their organisation and to the subject. Training materials, especially case studies, should be 'customised' (that is based on the employer's own practice and workplace) as much as possible, indeed you may have to write your own or adapt existing material.

Components of equality training

The three main components in equality training are raising awareness through education, giving knowledge leading to greater understanding and giving skills and experience.

Do not try to expose and challenge people's attitudes and values, and do not try to change attitudes directly. Such training, which has been tried under various types of 'racism' or 'sexism awareness', will not succeed except in very specialised circumstances, involving intensive one-to-one or small group counselling. It is suitable only for staff who already have very high levels of awareness and experience, for example, counsellors or equal opportunity staff. Your aim should be to influence (and eventually change) attitudes, by education and by changing behaviour.

Change in behaviour is a gradual process, which starts with people becoming aware of the need for change, because they recognise that there is a gap between what they do or say, and external circumstances such as how others respond. People want to change when this gap becomes too wide for comfort; when they feel 'out of step' or 'left behind'. But change in behaviour will only be maintained if it is reinforced by the organisation and the people in it. That is why it is important for equality training to be set in context; it can help bring about change, but it cannot be the driving agent. It is also why your training objectives need to be realistically defined. You, your company, and above all, your course participants need to be clear what to expect from the training, and have a basis for judging whether the objective was achieved.

At the simplest level, all your staff need to be aware of your equal opportunities policy, the law and what these mean for their actions at work. They also need to know about the reasons for the policy, and the extent and effect of race and sex discrimination. At the most detailed level, staff who specialise in personnel management, selection or training, need skills as well as knowledge. The scope of each component is set out below.

Education and awareness training:

- the nature and extent of prejudice and discrimination – culture and value systems;
- the effects of prejudice and discrimination on its victims (over/under reacting, opting out, anti-social behaviour);
- negative responses to unfamiliar behaviour (ridicule, denial, rejection, blame the victim);
- the historical effects of systems;
- the law and company policy.

Knowledge and understanding:

- knowledge of the law – direct and indirect discrimination;
- identifying discriminatory mechanisms and barriers;
- identifying neutral processes and removing disparate effects;
- identifying solutions to under-achievement;
- monitoring and evaluation – interpreting, using and presenting data, and measuring performance;
- identifying appropriate working patterns and facilities for access;
- identifying problems caused by cultural, racial or sex differences.

Skills

- counselling;
- challenging discriminatory, racial or sexist behaviour, or expressed prejudices in staff and/or customers;
- knowing what information is needed from interviews and how to recognise behavioural differences;
- assessment – how to use information in decisions and overcome behavioural differences;
- managing diversity
  building multi-racial teams
  accommodating and using value and cultural differences
  strengthening performance through diversity
  dealing with conflict and communication barriers

---

cultural and gender differences in giving and receiving negative feedback.

Planning and setting up equal opportunities training

Effective equal opportunities training requires a systematic method of identifying training needs, setting objectives, selecting training methods and finally an evaluation or review of the training given. You will need to cost and plan it within your budget.

The training must be relevant to your departmental needs and to the managerial objectives for equal opportunities, and it must meet individual managers' needs.

The type of training to be given must be planned in priority order, again, to be consistent with your equal opportunity objectives and departmental needs.

There are seven stages in planning and setting up equal opportunities training, in common with any other training:

- organisational context
- training needs analysis;
- defining objectives and standards;
- preparing programmes/content and materials;
- trainer training/preparations;
- trainee – selection;
- evaluation and monitoring.

The organisational context

In planning training, you need to find answers to the following questions.

- Where and how does the training fit in with the equal opportunities strategy (see Chapter 2)? Is it needed and will it help get results?
- Where and how does the EO training fit in with other training, such as recruitment and staff development, or management training. Is it relevant and does it help managers do their jobs?
- Who has to be released by whom? Have their managers been prepared? Will they benefit (from more effective managers, better recruitment or better staff relationships)?
- Practical considerations such as when, where and from whose budget must also be decided.

Most equality training should be integral to mainstream management training. For example, it could be a module in your selection or appraisal training, or any personnel management or management development training. At the beginning of a new equality initiative, such as a change in practices or a new strategic plan, it will also be necessary to arrange stand-alone equality training to raise awareness or get things started. Apart from new events, however, it is recommended that equality training should not be as a stand-alone. If it is undertaken as separate or specialised training, equal opportunities will be seen as marginal, or for someone else, and not as a matter for all managers of staff.

Training needs analysis

In designing training, you must be clear what the training is for, and what particular needs are to be met. The answer will depend on the level of staff, their function and the stage of equal opportunity development your company has reached. The same questions will arise whatever the scale; that is, if you are training for a department, section, plant or company.

Some questions to ask in identifying needs

	Training need
Top managers	
1. Do they support equality initiatives with: ● action, directives/instructions ● resources ● up the line (to board level)?	understanding, awareness
2. Are they aware of recent equality initiatives?	
3. Do they have a recruitment or staff development or training policy? Does the company have secondment or retention problems or anticipate skill shortages?	
4. Do they give equality action high priority?	
5. Do they hold their subordinates accountable for progress, e.g. through performance appraisals, reviews of key results?	
6. Do they use monitoring data when compiling business plans and to inform strategic plans?	
Managers and supervisors	
1. Do they know about the equality legislation and what it means for them in daily decision making?	
2. Can they identify some common ways in which discrimination occurs in the company?	

(continued)

3. Do they have direct responsibility for implementing the equality programme?	understanding awareness
4. Can they suggest how to deal with discrimination and a timescale?	specific skills
5. Are they accountable for results? Is their performance measured?	information

6. Do they have a specific equal opportunities objective in their own job plans?
   Is there an action plan relating to equal opportunities?
7. What results have they achieved? Are they satisfied with these? Are there barriers not tackled?
8. Do they feel equality problems are for someone else to solve?
9. Do they feel equality programmes create problems or add to their work?
10. Do they record decisions and reasons, and use monitoring data to set targets or review results?
11. What relevant training have they attended? In what ways did it change their actions?
12. What priority do they give to equal opportunities? What other tasks/pressures have prevented progress?
13. Do they communicate equal opportunity objectives and plans to staff?
14. Are their staff aware of the grievance procedure?
15. Do their staff have particular problems? Are they evading the issue or failing to challenge 'difficult' colleagues?
16. Have they had complaints/disputes/incidents in which race or sex discrimination was alleged?
17. Have they operated flexible working arrangements? Placed people with disabilities?
18. Do they have problems with recruitment or retention? Or a lack of skills or staff with ability for promotion?

Personnel Staff
1. Do they know the company's equal opportunity strategy, goals and procedures?
2. Do they know the main points in the equality legislation and equality Codes of Practice (issued by CRE, EOC and Department of Employment for people with disabilities)?

3. Do they know about bias-free recruitment
   selection and assessment methods?
4. Can they use monitoring data to identify
   barriers and advise managers on good
   equality practices, and setting and using
   targets?
5. Do they know where and when postive action
   (encouragement and training) is appropriate
   to the company?
6. Do they know how to apply grievance and
   disciplinary procedures to racial and sexual
   harassment, and to counsel individuals?

Line Employees
1. Do they know of and understand the company
   equal opportunities policy? Have they ever
   discussed it with colleagues?
2. Have they/would they use the grievance
   process on an equality issue?
   Do they know their EO officer?
3. Do they believe the policy is working?
   If not/why not?
4. Have they applied for promotion or training
   opportunities?
   If not, why not?
5. Is the office free of racist or sexist jokes?
   Or resentment about the policy or free of a
   belief that standards have been lowered?

Two or more 'no' answers to the above indicate a training need. The
following objectives relate back to areas identified in your training
analysis, and should also be related to the overall priorities of your
equality programme.

Training objectives

These are some of the training objectives which relate to the analysis
at each level of staff.

Top managers:

- awareness of their legal and company accountability and
  weak points in their organisation (practices and where there
  is any under-representation);

- ability to formulate strategic plans for equal opportunities;
- making their managers responsible;
- using key indicators for measuring performance in equal opportunities.

Line managers:

- awareness of their legal and company responsibility and effect on decisions/actions;
- knowledge of barriers and solutions;
- skills for dealing with inter-cultural and sex differences and giving feedback;
- skills for managing diversity;
- knowledge and skills for getting the best out of staff from different backgrounds;
- interviewing, counselling and assessment skills for managers who recruit, promote or assess staff performance;
- knowledge of departmental staff profile – how to set and use targets and measure results;
- ability to challenge discriminatory behaviour.

Personnel staff:

- knowledge of company policy, strategy and programmes;
- awareness of legal framework and equality codes of practice;
- knowledge of barriers and bias-free recruitment, selection and assessment practices;
- ability to interpret monitoring data, understanding and use of simple statistical tests and ways to measure progress (e.g. use of goals and targets);
- knowledge of relevant methods to encourage under-represented groups and appropriate use of positive action training;
- knowledge of appropriate procedures and counselling techniques.

Line employees:

- awareness and understanding of reasons for equality policies and the objectives;
- understanding of concepts;
- encouragement to participate in development and apply for promotion;
- understanding how to create non-racist, non-sexist working relationships.

MAKING EQUAL OPPORTUNITIES WORK

The preceding sections outline ways of identifying training needs at different levels and functions and give suggested objectives for this training. But much equality training fails to meet managers' or an organisation's needs because it is too generalised and insufficiently focused on improving competencies or understanding. This is partly because equality has been seen as a 'social' issue, incapable of precision. But your equality training must be effective and relevant to your business or organisations and directed towards improving efficiency. For this you need to be able to define achievements and performance standards. These can be set by tests and observations of trainees, during and after training, and by validation reports. Validation and evaluation is dealt with later in this chapter. Here we suggest some performance measures which can be tested during and after training. Your training materials and methods need to be directed towards making sure that trainees can reach these outcomes.

Trainee competance guidelines	Senior managers	Line managers	Personnel managers
Legislation and company policy			
Knowledge			
recall main points in equality legislation and Disabled Persons Employment Act and Codes of Practice	●	●	●
recall main points of company policy and own accountability	●	●	●
Understanding			
explain, with examples, how indirect discrimination and under-representation can occur	●	●	●
identify barriers in a case study and show how these are relevant to his/her own functions		●	●
identify solutions which would remove disparities; with a timetable for implementation		●	●

(continued)

Trainee competance guidelines	Senior managers	Line managers	Personnel managers
Action			
has informed line staff of policy		•	
can explain policy objectives orally to staff		•	
has set up system for progress reviews, and has set up targets	•	•	•
Managing diversity			
Understanding			
can identify individual behaviours in different cultures			
can recognise how cultural factors affect perceptions			
can identify prejudiced behaviour		•	•
Skills			
can provide counselling and negative feedback without causing resentment		•	•
can identify evidence about performance and analyse individual training and development needs			
can persuade others of the need for action			•
Selection and assessment			
Understanding			
can recognise discriminatory practices and communication barriers		•	•
can identify discriminatory behaviour		•	•
can identify interview techniques and circumstances in which these are used		•	•
can distinguish between facts and assumptions		•	•
Action			
can demonstrate various		•	•

Trainee competence guidelines	Senior managers	Line managers	Personnel managers
types of interview questions			
can demonstrate listening and interviewing skills and overcome communication barriers		●	●
can obtain evidence about interviewees' performance and achievements		●	●
demonstrates how to evaluate facts against selection criteria		●	●
demonstrates how to identify and evaluate signs of under-achievement		●	●
Measuring equality opportunity performance			
Understanding			
understands the use of statistical measurement and its limitations		●	●
understands the main statistical measures available		●	●
Action			
can demonstrate how to identify key information in statistical presentations		●	●
can draw inferences and identify where management action is needed	●		●

Training content and materials

It is not possible to supply a blueprint for a training course, nor a list of suitable 'off-the-shelf' materials. As with all training, it is most effective when participants try out the necessary skills or gain the necessary knowledge from direct experience. Such experience must relate as closely as possible to real life and the workplace. If possible, use your company's specific examples for preparing case studies. Use your own

Table 7.1 Training plan: Summary of stages

Staff level	Training content	Objectives	EO stage
Board top managers	Knowledge and awareness of issues, legal and company role	Get support and leadership	Before adopting action programme
Line managers	Knowledge and awareness	Get support and ownership	First stage
	Understanding and recognising barriers		Second stage
	Changing diversity	Get action	Third stage
	Managing diversity	Get action	
	Evaluating/measuring performance	Increase pace of change	Fourth stage
	Positive action	Deal with effects of past	Fifth stage
Line staff	Awareness and understanding of policy	Get support	Second stage
	Creating a non-racist, non-sexist working environment	Get ownership	Fourth and fifth stage

MAKING EQUAL OPPORTUNITIES WORK

experience, or ask your colleagues and staff about a problem which they have had to solve, or an incident they have had to deal with, or look for examples of complaints. Use these either to write your own case studies or for role play (but do not do this in any way which identifies or allows others to identify the people involved.) What this means is that effective training must be:

● experienced-based;
● participative;
● replicate the workplace;
● be realistic;
● produce results in a positive climate.

Training materials which meet these principles must be 'customised', based on problems met by the organisation. Methods include:

● role-play;
● case studies for problem solving;
● in-tray exercises for bringing up equal opportunities into daily decision-taking;
● group discussions to enable participants to share experience;
● work on solving a common problem, and interpreting and generalising from their training experience;
● action planning to use the experience and apply to the trainee's own work place;
● structured on-the-job training.

You need to encourage trainees to discuss the issues as openly as possible, and you need to build opportunities for this into your course. This does not mean allowing unstructured open-ended or abstract discussions about people's opinions or feelings; this will simply cause people to retreat and keep their views to themselves. The best way of involving people in facing up to and thinking about equality is through small groups, carrying out activities such as solving problems in case studies, which demonstrate the practical issues involved. These allow people to discuss solutions without taking too much risk by disclosing too much of their own views.

Evaluation

There are a range of sophisticated techniques which can be used for evaluating the effectiveness of training on behaviour. Here we suggest a rough and ready method which will help you judge adequately whether the training was useful and achieved its objectives.

The first questionnaire should be given out immediately after the training has been completed. The follow-up questionnaire must be given six to nine months later, the same time as you give a questionnaire to the trainee's manager.

Initial questionnaire Questions to the superior officer	Follow-up six months later
1. Which changes did you find most useful and why? (decisions, promotions, outcomes, skills.)	Describe how this was helpful in the last six months.
2. Which did you find least useful and why?	
3. Were any of your needs not met?	
4. Describe what action you will take as a result of the training.	Did you take this action? If not, why not?
5. Identify what changes you will make in your working standards and decision-making.	Did you make these changes? What was the result? If not, why not?
6. What outcomes do you expect to achieve in six months/a year?	Did you achieve these outcomes? If not, why not?

The results will enable you to identify gaps in understanding or knowledge. This will tell you that you will need to spend more training time on these aspects. The answers will also help you assess what action is needed to improve your equal opportunities strategy. For example, if trainees were unable to make the changes which they planned because of opposition or lack of support from others, this indicates some senior management support or instructions are needed. If the changes were not made because of other priorities or lack of resources, this also suggests you need to review your departmental or company priorities, again with senior management support. If changes did not occur because company practices have not changed in line with the equal opportunity policy, you need to press those with 'ownership' – senior managers or personnel staff, or the unions, to get the changes, and revise your training priorities.

Positive action/developmental training

An essential component of an effective equal opportunities programme is training of under-represented groups – women, ethnic minorities and people with disabilities – to help overcome the effects of past discrimination and disadvantage. Put simply, your equal opportunities programme will not achieve an increase in the numbers of women or ethnic minorities at high levels, especially in management, unless your company is prepared to invest in this training. We know from research, and from looking at the long-term results of well-established equal opportunity programmes, that there is a cut-off point beyond which women and ethnic minority people do not progress. Often it has been argued that because women and ethnic minority employees have come into careers and management only relatively recently; with the passage of time, and given equal opportunity policies and non-discriminatory promotion, they will enter senior levels. But the evidence does not support this argument. Known as the 'glass ceiling', it appears that organisational cultures at the top of the pyramid, the effects of stereo-typed attitudes about who 'fits' at senior levels and the consequences of domestic pressures on women mean that senior levels are over-whelmingly white and male. Similar barriers exist in access to particular areas (e.g. production and engineering). One major reason for this is the tendency for us all to select people who look and think like us. But if more women and ethnic minorities had the skills, experience and confidence to compete equally, this would begin to change decision-making. One important step is to introduce an accelerated development programme, with training geared to meeting needs which have held these groups back. Unless this becomes part of your equal opportunity programme, there will not be sufficient numbers of under-represented groups there to reach the top; they will be unable to compete without this effort to overcome past disadvantage.

There are many other examples of positive action training. Some has been aimed at training applicants who lack particular skills. Pre-employment training has been called variously 'access training' and 'customised training', as well as 'positive action training'. Training has been open to all under-achievers with a common training need; some has been specific to women or particular racial groups. Whichever method is used, the clear purpose has been to enable people from under-represented groups to acquire skills or experience which would help them compete on the same or similar footing as white males. It is an investment in realising the untapped potential in the labour market.

The main components of this training have included:

● developing and enriching basic oral and written language skills;

- researching, preparing and presenting papers, submissions, proposals or plans;
- numeracy;
- presentational skills;
- chairing and contributing to meetings;
- effective administrative/office skills/telephone skills;
- social and life skills;
- basic vocational skills, for example using keyboards, cash registers, customer service and care, technical drawings;
- training for access to particular professions (e.g. housing management, environmental health, financial services, banking, nursing, data processing);
- supervisory and management skills.

There have also been a wide range of courses aimed at developing women's management potential. (Similar courses may be run for ethnic minorities and people with disabilities). A typical course has included the following:

Women's only management training: model course outline

Issues covered

Personal career analysis	–identifying likes and dislikes/decisions made and why/matching work and domestic responsibilities
Personal strengths and weaknesses	–assertiveness training/negotiating skills/presentational skills/participating in and chairing meetings
Organisational structures	–understanding how the organisation operates/identifying career paths/understanding where the individual course member's job/section fits in to the organisational structure
Equal Opportunity Policies at work	–understanding discrimination/ understanding the company's equal opportunity policies
Positive use of power	–personal power/expert power/positional power/organisation power
Dealing with stress and pressure at work	–combining work and domestic responsibilities/dealing with sexual harassment/managing stress
Forward career planning	–identifying a career development plan

The benefits of positive action training

Employee development or pre-employment training has found some important benefits to offer.

- It can be a cost-effective way of meeting skill or labour shortages.
- It improves the company image and the credibility of equal opportunity policies. Within a two to three-year time-span, it has increased the numbers of qualified ethnic minority or women candidates applying to companies.
- It produces tangible, measurable results.
- It can improve selection, because of its emphasis on essential skills and experience. In some companies this has demonstrated a gap between those needed for the job, and selection criteria, resulting in a review of selection.
- It can lead to improved employee development. In some organisations, the identification of key skills and pre-employment positive action training programme has been successfully modified to meet the needs of internal staff. This resulted in improved career opportunities and avoided a build-up of resentment at an external training programme for minorities or women.

Before considering any investment in this training, it is essential to make sure that there is no unnecessary selection barrier. Otherwise the training will be a waste of money.

As with manager training, positive action or access training must follow the same planning and needs analysis as other training.

Identifying positive action training needs

Look at a sample of about 50 unsuccessful candidates for jobs in your company. Compare their experience and skills against successful candidates and the job needs. Make a list of the skills or experience which is missing and compare whites with ethnic minorities, and men and women. Identify gaps as a basis for defining needs.

Interview samples of failed candidates to find out their perceptions and experience of the selection process covering such aspects as:

- Whether they felt confident or comfortable and if not why?
- Their knowledge of the job requirements.
- Their thoughts about any training needs.
- Their willingness to attend training.

Example

Job skills	Gaps	Training
Report writing	ability to set out logical arguments	problem solving tables to identify components
	use of clear precise expression	reading and writing and comprehension
		exercises to enrich use of language and ability to use
		understanding formal informal/direct/in- direct speech and expressions

- Their circumstances (i.e. to help design when and where training should be undertaken).
- Their long-term aspirations (to help assess training relevance and objectives).

Also, interview selectors to find out their perceptions of why ethnic minority, or women or disabled candidates failed to reach standards. And, interview trainers to find out about their experience of the training needed, to identify trainer training and any missing experiences.

Then, use all the information gained to define basic principles for the training, the component elements, ranked in priority, and the methods. If you have time and can bring in candidates, draw up work samples or 'tasters' for candidates to try out some of the tasks involved. This will help confirm whether you have identified all training needs at the correct levels and extent. Your training course can be adjusted to give more emphasis to aspects which need to be strengthened.

Should the training be specific to women, or black and Asian people?

Positive action training (see Chapter 1) exclusively for ethnic minority people has been rarely used. Examples include the BBC Asian and Afro-Caribbean Reporters' Trust (to bring ethnic minority reporters to BBC TV and radio news), and PATH (Positive Action in Training and Housing) to bring ethnic minorities into housing departments and associations, later extended to other vocational areas of local government. There have been many more examples of women-only training (e.g. Barclays Bank's scheme to bring more women into management).

Racially-specific training has been much more difficult to sell to senior managers and staff, and you will meet more resentment and opposition than if you start with a mixed group. It will therefore take longer to get agreement to funding, and will take longer to set up because you will first have to get the support and understanding of trainers and personnel staff. One solution is to design training which meets similar needs of other disadvantaged people, those starting a second career, women returners or the unemployed. But if the barriers mainly affect ethnic minority candidates, and if they are under-represented in the work concerned, make sure that their numbers in training are sufficient to increase entry levels and help reduce under-representation. You can do this by ranking candidates according to need.

Managing positive action training

Examination of employers who already run positive action training suggests that there are some key management principles to be followed in ensuring its success. These are that:

- senior management must be consulted during the design and delivery of training, giving them the chance to influence content and quality control;
- experienced trainers must be used to deliver the training (but their skills or methods may need to be developed as suggested above);
- training must be 'customised' and as close to the workplace as possible;
- training must be focused at a clear objective with objectively measurable levels of achievement. As already indicated, these must relate to your company's needs, and link in with existing training, and accreditation or promotion fields;
- monitoring and evaluation must be built in, both to training, and to the subsequent progress of trainees, in comparison with progress of staff generally.

EXAMPLES OF POSITIVE ACTION TRAINING FOR ETHNIC MINORITIES

1. *The PATH training scheme*

   PATH Yorkshire Ltd was established in 1985, to provide vocational training and education for people from ethnic minorities in the Leeds, Bradford, Kirklees and Sheffield areas. The first scheme was for entry to housing management. In 1986, PATH organised a 60-place 2 year rolling programme with Leeds City Council, to encourage more ethnic minorities into administration. Subsequent schemes included training for entry to legal services, building, highways, architectural technicianships and laboratory technicianships. In 1987, three 12 month training schemes were established to encourage entry into business, including retail management and financial services.

2. *Project COMTRAN Ltd – Bradford*

Project Comtran Ltd was set up to offer traineeship to young people from ethnic minorities to provide training and 12 month work placements, leading to management or a profession. Companies providing placements included Lloyds Bank, Trustee Savings Bank, Halifax Building Society, Asda Stores, National Westminster Bank and West Yorkshire Probation Service.

3. *London Weekend Television*

In 1991 LWT started offering traineeships for people from ethnic minorities, to train for the freelance market as assistants in sound and camera. The company also offers bursaries for ethnic minority students on the main post-graduate journalism courses and extended work attachments in corporate affairs press, publicity and entertainments. None of these measures are for the trainees to work for LWT, but are to help increase the pool of qualified people from ethnic minorities in the broadcasting industry.

4. *The Windsor Fellowship*

The Windsor Fellowship was set up in 1986 to encourage, support and prepare undergraduates from ethnic minority communities for management careers in industry, commerce and public administration. The fellowship targets young people, mainly from inner city schools, who have been offered a place on a degree course. Fellows are supported by an employer, with whom they spend two periods of work experience. The fellowship runs seminars on management skills and personal and team development, to help fellows maximise their potential and develop as role models. Fellows also give 2 hours a week to voluntary work. Employers benefit from an opportunity to identify well qualified ethnic minority employees and the scheme offers a way of turning equal opportunity policies into action.

To summarise, training is an essential component of an equal opportunities strategy, but will only be effective if it is planned and its scope and objectives clearly defined, based on your organisation's, and individual participant's, needs. Your training should concentrate on obtaining realistic results, and you should check whether these goals have been attained by carrying out a follow-up survey. Finally, don't overlook the need for developmental training for those groups that have fallen behind because of the effects of discrimination and earlier disadvantage.

- analyse what equality training is appropriate to your organisation, taking into account the equal opportunity programme;
- identify priorities and levels (or grades) for training;
- analyse training needs of each level;
- identify training objectives, methods and standards;
- prepare course content and materials;
- prepare/brief trainers;
- select trainees;
- after training, evaluate the effectiveness.

CHAPTER 8
Working Arrangements

Industry and commerce loses the skills, knowledge and experience of a large proportion of the women in the workforce because it fails to offer the working arrangements that enable people to cope with both work and domestic responsibilities effectively. By establishing a package of more flexible working patterns, good parental leave arrangements, facilities for short career breaks and help with childcare arrangements, employers can retain more staff and avoid the costs of a high turnover rate, recruit from a wider section of the labour force and achieve greater equality for men and women at work.

This chapter looks at how to go about establishing greater flexibility in working arrangement and at the benefits that this can offer both the employer and employees. It is not intended as a detailed and comprehensive guide to setting up, for example, a workplace nursery or a scheme for homeworking. The purpose is to provide a starting point and framework for deciding which schemes will work best for you and how to begin introducing such schemes.

Flexible working pattern

Different working patterns are already common; many people undertake shift work, some industries are characterised by part-time working, and in certain sectors of the economy contract employment is the norm. However, certain working patterns are often seen to be appropriate only for certain types of work. While it is common to find part-time cleaners it is less usual to find a part-time doctor or lawyer. In some cases the demands of the work mean that one kind of working pattern is more efficient than another but, more often, working patterns are simply a result of tradition and convention.

More and more employers are, however, beginning to make use of the flexibility that modern technology provides and to look at working patterns more imaginatively in order to make the best use of their staff and other resources. In the computer industry, for example, companies such as ICL and the FI Group have developed opportunities for home working – the FI Group operates almost entirely on the basis of 'remote working'. In the civil service, flexible working hours are widely available and part-time working is now common at senior management levels, as well as at more junior grades. Retail companies such as Dixons and Boots have pioneered opportunities for 'term-time' working – a working pattern which allows people with school-age children to work during school term-times and to take a 'break' from paid employment during school holidays. The major clearing banks such as National Westminster, Barclay's and Midland have well established career break schemes that enable staff to take time away from work when their children are young with a guarantee of a return to work. Experience shows that flexible working patterns can work successfully to the benefit of both management and staff in a wide variety of different jobs and at all management levels.

Introducing flexible working patterns

The kinds of flexible working arrangements that are likely to be of most benefit in achieving greater equality at work are:

- flexible working hours;
- part-time working and job-sharing;
- home-working;
- term-time working; and
- for people with severe disabilities, sheltered placement.

If you are introducing these kinds of arrangements for the first time, you will need to:

- work out how the new flexible working arrangements will operate;
- set up the new schemes in consultation with trade union or staff representatives and if necessary, run a pilot scheme;
- publicise the new arrangements within your organisation and in your recruitment literature; and
- monitor the new arrangements.

Working out the scheme

FLEXIBLE WORKING HOURS
The system of flexible working hours is now a well-established working

pattern in many organisations. It is simple and straight forward to set up and operate. Staff work the usual contracted hours but, within certain limits, are able to vary their arrival and departure times and are able to 'bank' extra hours worked and take time off in lieu at a later date. This kind of flexibility is popular with staff and can be particularly helpful to:

- staff with children who may wish to arrive later in the morning or leave earlier in the afternoon to collect children from school, nurseries or childminders;
- staff caring for elderly relatives who may similarly need flexibility in their arrival and departure times;
- staff with disabilities who may welcome the opportunity to travel to work out of rush hour;
- staff who may wish to take time away from work to attend events during the working day.

Flexible working hours arrangements operate on the basis of a core period, a daily accounting period, a weekly or monthly accounting period and carry-over time.

Core period

Although staff can vary the time at which they arrive and leave work, most flexible working hours arrangements have a 'core period' during the day within which all staff must be in the office, except when they are taking lunch. Typically the core period is between the hours of 10 a.m. and 4 p.m. This ensures that during the period of the day when most business is done, staff are available on the telephone, for meetings or for discussions, at the same time as allowing staff flexibility as to when they carry out their remaining contracted hours.

Daily accounting period

Staff may arrive and leave at times outside the core hours on any day. However, it is usual to place a limit on the times within which hours worked will count as flexible working hours. This is the daily accounting period. For example, the flexible working hours system may operate for a twelve hour period during the day – say 7 a.m. to 7 p.m. Staff can arrive and leave at any time within this daily accounting period and outside the core hours. So, if the core period is 10 a.m.–4 p.m., staff may arrive anytime between 7 and 10 a.m. and leave any time between 4 and 7 p.m. The maximum number of hours that can be worked on 'flexi-time' in a day is 12 hours.

The setting of a daily accounting period ensures that managers have some control over when staff work, both during the day and over the week. From the staff's point of view it allows overtime arrangements and flexible working hours arrangements to operate side by side. Any hours worked before or after the daily accounting period will be treated as overtime in the usual way.

Weekly or monthly accounting period

The weekly or monthly accounting period provides a basis for managers to monitor hours worked and provides a framework within which staff can take extra days away from work by working longer hours over a period of days. Most flexible working hour arrangements operate on the basis of a four week accounting period. At the end of four weeks staff are provided with a statement of the number of hours worked, set against the number of contracted hours. This enables staff to see whether they are in credit or in debit for the month.

Carry-over time

At the end of every monthly accounting period, hours in credit are carried over into the next accounting period. The extra hours can be taken as 'flexi-leave' during the next accounting period; this is in addition to the usual annual leave allowance. It is usually also possible for staff to 'borrow' time to take as flexi-leave during an accounting period such that at the end of the period they may be in debit on the number of hours worked.

There is normally, however, a maximum number of hours that staff are able to carry over or 'borrow' somewhere between the equivalent of one and three days. Again, this allows managers control over when and for what period staff can take time away from work in lieu of the extra hours worked.

Monitoring hours worked

In order to operate a flexible working system effectively, staff need to keep an accurate record of the hours they have worked. There are many computer operated systems on the market to enable this to be done easily and efficiently. They depend on a 'clocking in' or 'keying in' system and each member of staff is issued with a personalised 'key' or 'pass-card'. However, less formal systems also operate whereby staff keep a written record of the hours worked and monitoring is undertaken by local management. Whatever mechanism is adopted the basic arrangements are the same. A record is kept of the time of arrival, time at which lunch break begins, time at which lunch break ends and time of leaving work at the end of the day.

Conditions of service
There are few, if any, implications for terms and conditions of employment. Practical arrangements need to be set up to take account of absences on leave, on sick leave, to visit the dentist or doctor, or to attend a meeting outside of the office. This can be done by a written update to be submitted to the manager of the flexible working hours system.

PART-TIME WORKING, JOB SHARING, HOME-WORKING, TERM-TIME WORKING

Part-time working, job sharing, home-working and term-time working are working patterns that provide people with the flexibility to cope effectively with both work and home. They have traditionally been treated as different from full-time work, attracting different conditions of service and different contracts. For flexible working patterns to contribute effectively to an equal opportunity policy, however, it is essential that:

- conditions of service are as good as those offered full-time employees;
- there is flexibility for staff to shift between different working patterns at different stages in their careers;
- as far as is practicable, opportunities for flexible working are available at all management levels and across all types of job; and
- flexible working patterns are seen to make a legitimate and valuable contribution to work.

Here are some of the points you should consider.

Pay rates
Pay rates should be equivalent to pay rates for undertaking the job on a full-time basis. For part-time working, job-sharing and term-time working this simply means full-time pay on a pro-rata basis; for home-working you may need to consider a different rate of pay to take account of the expense of working at home. This can also be done through expenses payments.

London weighting
Companies that pay an allowance to those working in London will

need to consider how to deal with this – for part-time workers and job-sharers it may be appropriate to pay the full allowance, particularly to those who travel to work each day and therefore have the same travel and living expenses as a full-time worker. In the case of home-workers, you may wish to base eligibility for London weighting on the location of the member of staff's home.

Pensions

All flexible working hours should accrue pension rights. Make sure that your pension scheme can accommodate a range of working patterns and that, for example, job-sharing that involves working one week on/one week off does not constitute a break in employment continuity. Similar considerations apply to term-time working.

Holidays

Home-workers should qualify for holidays in the same way as site workers. Part-time staff, job-sharers and term-time workers should qualify for holidays on a pro-rata basis.

Expenses/insurance/company cars

This is mainly relevant to home-workers. You will need to decide how you will reimburse staff for telephone charges and other expenses associated with work. You will also need to ensure that any equipment necessary for the job is properly insured. Where a part-time worker is eligible for a company car, you will need to consider how this should be treated. The solution may differ, depending on whether the car is essential for performing the job or is part of an overall remuneration package.

Training

If you have flexible working patterns you also need to provide flexible training arrangements. Many part-time staff will be able to attend short full-time training courses, but modular courses and distance learning packages can also be helpful.

Home-working for people with disabilities

Because of a debilitating accident, or through illness, some people may find it impossible to travel to work, even though they are quite capable of carrying out the work required of them. The Department of Employment operates a special scheme that provides financial support to employers who recruit or employ staff who, because of a disability,

MAKING EQUAL OPPORTUNITIES WORK

are prevented from travelling to work. The scheme is called the Remote Working Scheme. Financial assistance is provided under the scheme for any special equipment that the member of staff may need to work from home. In all other respects such disabled workers are treated like any other home worker. Information about the scheme can be obtained from the Disablement Advisory Service contactable through your local job centre.

SHELTERED PLACEMENTS

Sheltered placement is also a pattern of employment funded through the Department of Employment and designed specifically to meet the needs of people with a severe disability. The objective of the scheme is to encourage open employment for people whose disability is so severe as to prevent them undertaking a fully loaded job. For the employer it provides an opportunity both to retain staff who may become severely disabled as a result of accident or illness and to recruit from a pool of potential employees who would otherwise be outside the usual recruitment pool.

The kind of people who may be recruited under the sheltered employment scheme may be people who have a physical disability such that it slows significantly the speed at which they can work or they may have learning difficulties and only be able to undertake certain simple tasks. Given the right employment conditions they have a valuable contribution to make.

The sheltered placement scheme involves:

- the disabled worker;
- the host employer who provides a job;
- a sponsoring organisation who is the legal employer of the disabled worker;
- Department of Employment which provides funding for the scheme through the sponsoring organisation.

It operates quite simply. The host employer provides a job. The sponsoring organisation (a voluntary organisation or a local authority) identifies a suitable worker. The output of the worker in the particular job on offer is assessed. If it appears that the worker is say capable of 60% of the output normally expected, then an agreement is reached such that the host organisation pays 60% of the worker's wages and the sponsoring organisation pays the other 40%. The scheme is co-ordinated by the Department of Employment's Disablement Advisory Service, who produce a leaflet which tells you more about it. They will also give help and advice on involvement in the scheme. Your local job centre will be able to provide you with the address of your nearest disablement advisory service office.

Setting up the scheme

In a company that is unused to working patterns other than full-time, you are likely to meet resistance to the introduction of new flexible working patterns. Here are some of the objections you may meet:

- part-time working won't work – someone needs to be available all the time;
- it's impossible to manage staff as a part-time worker or home-worker, it's not fair on junior staff;
- it's impossible to manage a home-worker, how will I know what work is being done and how will I assess performance?;
- part-time working is expensive, we need twice as many desks, phones, etc.;
- job sharing won't work, it's too difficult to match people and what happens if one-half of the job share leaves?;
- if everyone works flexitime, they will stay at work to build up time when there is nothing for them to do and take time off when it is essential for them to be there;
- other staff won't be prepared to work alongside someone working on a sheltered placement arrangement, it will put an extra burden on other staff.

Experience of flexible working patterns is the best way to dispel such doubts. You can also point to the positive aspects:

- part-time working can help to achieve more balanced work loads by, for example, enabling a heavily loaded full-time job to be split into one full-time and one part-time job;
- having flexible working patterns doesn't mean that an office is unstaffed, it simply means that different people are there at different times;
- a part-time boss provides junior staff with the opportunity to take more responsibility for their own work and to become involved in events that might otherwise be reserved for their manager;
- flexible working patterns can save money for the company by retaining staff, it can enable women to return from maternity leave at an earlier date and provide continuity in staffing.

MAKING EQUAL OPPORTUNITIES WORK

The kind of flexible working arrangements that will work best for your organisation will depend on the nature of the work, the needs of staff and the culture of the organisation. A staff survey and discussions with managers and with staff or trade union representatives can help decide the right scheme or schemes for your organisation. A pilot scheme can help iron out any practical difficulties that may arise and help demonstrate to sceptical managers that part-time working, home-working or flexible working hours is really viable.

If you are faced with resistance to flexible working arrangements try looking for sympathetic managers, areas where there are recruitment difficulties, areas where there is a heavy work load, areas which rely on computer technology making home-working an easy option to try, or areas where the nature of the work is particularly receptive to being broken down into smaller self-contained work loads (e.g. case work) or areas which are high profile and high status and will therefore ensure that flexible working patterns are visible.

Once the details of the scheme have been worked out, good written guidance will help ensure that staff and managers understand the scheme and use it effectively. Monitoring the way in which it works can provide the opportunity to resolve any unforseen difficulties that may arise. Good publicity for the scheme will help ensure that it is taken up throughout the rest of the organisation, and advertising it in recruitment literature can help attract applicants from a wide range of different backgrounds.

Improving parental leave arrangements and career breaks

Staff with children or other domestic commitments may need to take short or sometimes longer spells away from work at particular stages in their career. Examples are:

- those with babies;
- those with very young children;
- those adopting children;
- when children or other dependent relatives are ill; or
- those caring for an elderly relative.

Some people may also wish to take a career break to follow a course of study or some other short-term activity. Providing appropriate leave and career break arrangements can provide employers with the opportunity to 're-employ' such staff when their period out of paid employment ends.

There is already a statutory requirement to provide a period of maternity leave (see Employment Protection (Consolidation) Act 1978). But many employers are now offering:

- maternity leave enhanced beyond the statutory minimum – often up to a year part paid;
- paternity leave – for periods from 2–3 days up to 2–3 weeks;
- short-term paid leave – for periods of between 5–15 days available to staff who have to cope with a domestic crisis such as the sudden illness of a child or close relative;
- long-term career breaks with a right of return.

The third action programme of the European Commission recognises the need for more measures to help men and women reconcile working and family life.

Long-term career breaks

The idea of providing staff with the opportunity to take a number of years away from work when their children are small was pioneered by the large clearing banks, in particular the National Westminster Bank, and by the civil service. The objective is to provide a structure and framework for such absences and effective keeping-in-touch arrangements to ensure that contact with the employee is not lost and that employees have the opportunity to maintain their skill level and familiarity with the organisation. Many other employers now provide a similar facility. The essential features of career break arrangements is:

- a right of return to work at the same level at which the member of staff left the organisation;
- absence away from work for a maximum and fixed period of time;
- a commitment from the employer to provide the absent member of staff with information about new developments at work and with the opportunity for regular periods of work experience; and
- a commitment from the absent member of staff to participate in the work experience activities that form part of the keeping in touch arrangements.

Career break schemes of this kind are simple and cheap to set up and run and can make a real contribution to retaining staff in the long term. In setting up a scheme of this kind you need to decide on the following issues.

THE LENGTH OF ABSENCE YOU ARE GOING TO OFFER

Most existing schemes offer career breaks of up to five years to cover the pre-school years, with the opportunity to return to work at an earlier stage. After an absence from work of this period of time it may not be easy to find an appropriate job for the returning member of staff at short notice. It is therefore useful to build into your scheme a requirement to give, say, three or six months, notice of an intention to return to work or to build in an undertaking to find a suitable posting within six months of a request to return to work. Whether or not you do this it will be sensible to interview all those on career break schemes before the expected date of return in order to plan for this return.

WHAT HAPPENS TO ANY FINANCIAL BENEFITS

If your organisation offers any benefits etc. to staff, such as mortgages at low interest rates or membership of clubs, you will need to decide how to handle these during the career break period. The opportunity to retain a low interest mortgage will, for example, be an important incentive to the member of staff to return to work with your organisation. Continued membership of clubs or professional associations will help the absent member of staff to keep in touch with both social and professional events. You should also make arrangements to preserve pension rights and to ensure that when the member of staff does return to work, he or she is able to continue to accrue pension rights within the same scheme.

WHICH STAFF WILL BE ELIGIBLE

Some employers have chosen to make such schemes available to all staff, others have made the scheme available to those with a good attendance and performance record and others have limited the scheme to those who have been with the company for a minimum period of say two or three years. Some employers have schemes limited to staff wishing to take a break to look after children; others have included reasons such as further education. Whichever approach you adopt, it is important to remember that such schemes must be available to both men and women; to restrict eligibility to only one sex would be discriminatory within the terms of the Sex Discrimination Act 1975.

WHO WILL BE RESPONSIBLE FOR KEEPING IN TOUCH WITH THE ABSENT MEMBER OF STAFF

It is clearly essential for personnel departments to take the lead in running such schemes, but the personnel officer may not always be the best person to keep in touch. Where an organisation operates from a number of different sites or is made up of a number of small management units (e.g. banks, schools etc.) it may be more sensible for the local manager or for the member of staff's line manager to be responsible for maintaining contact with staff from his or her office. This will make it easier for absent staff to return to work, to attend social occasions etc., as well as keeping in touch in a more formal way through newsletters or interviews with personnel.

HOW TO KEEP IN TOUCH

There are many ways of keeping in touch with staff. Here are some examples:

- newsletters – either the organisation's regular newsletter or a special newsletter for those on career breaks;
- home visits – personnel staff may wish to make occasional visits to absent staff at their homes;
- update seminars – annual half-day seminars for those on career breaks provides an opportunity for staff both to keep in touch and be updated on new developments at work;
- office parties and other social occasions – inviting absent staff to social occasions helps them keep in touch with ex-colleagues and will help ensure that there is some familiarity about work when they eventually return;
- networks – fostering a network among those on career breaks can also be a helpful way of enabling people to keep in touch and feel that they are still part of the organisation;
- allow staff the opportunity to continue membership of sports and leisure clubs etc.

HOW TO HELP STAFF MAINTAIN THEIR SKILL LEVELS

Different approaches will be appropriate for different kinds of jobs. You may, for example:

- offer the opportunity to return to work for a period of two weeks or more each year – many employers do in fact require this commitment from staff as a condition of participating in the career break scheme, staff are of course paid for this time at work;
- invite staff to attend training courses, particularly where these are courses focusing on a new initiative or new regulations etc.;

- allow staff the opportunity to undertake work at home if this is appropriate, for example scientific and academic staff may wish to review papers or comment on the research work of their colleagues, and staff generally may be able to take on short projects that can arise from time to time;
- provide staff with access to libraries etc. at work so that they can visit and use these facilities as appropriate.

FACILITATING THE RETURN TO WORK

If keeping-in-touch arrangements have operated successfully the return to work should be well planned and the individual member of staff should feel confident and comfortable about coming back to the work environment. However, you may also wish to consider setting up a short 'induction' course and it may be helpful for personnel staff to keep in touch with returning staff for the first few months to resolve any difficulties that may arise.

PUBLICISING THE SCHEME

Clearly, if the scheme is to be successful it is important that all staff know of its existence and understand the way it works. You will therefore need to:

- discuss and explain the scheme to your trade union side;
- publicise the scheme in staff newsletters etc.;
- ensure that all personnel staff know about and understand the scheme;
- provide information about the scheme to all women taking maternity leave;
- publicise the scheme in recruitment literature;
- monitor the scheme and publicise information about the way it is operating.

Help with childcare arrangements

Flexible working patterns provide one way of enabling staff to combine work and domestic responsibilities effectively. However, as more and more women choose to combine work and motherhood, good quality, reliable and accessible childcare facilities are becoming an increasingly important issue for employers, and male and female employees alike. Many employers are therefore beginning to think seriously about the way they can contribute to childcare arrangements and about the benefits that this can provide for them and their staff. There are a number of different options. For example:

- a workplace nursery – a number of employers have chosen to invest in a nursery run on their own premises. Employers who pay corporation tax can get tax relief under the normal business tax rules for day-to-day expenditure on childcare provision for employees' children. The day-to-day running costs of a workplace nursery would qualify for such tax relief. Relief may also be given through the capital allowances system for certain capital expenditure on a workplace nursery. Advice and further information can be obtained from the Inland Revenue. There is statutory regulation of day nursery facilities. These are set out in the Children Act 1989. Minimum standards for nursery provision are set by local authorities and nursery provision must be registered with the local authority.
- a service to help employees find locally based and reliable childminders – personnel departments can research and put together a list of local childminders to help staff returning to work to find appropriate childcare arrangements and to help staff whose childcare arrangements break down to find a new childminder.
- childcare vouchers and childcare allowances – some employers have chosen to provide staff with children with a financial contribution towards childcare costs, this can be done simply by an extra payment to salary or by providing childcare vouchers in the same way as luncheon vouchers are provided;
- 'buying' places in locally run nurseries close to the place of employment – some, local nurseries may have unused places or may be prepared to take on staff to provide extra places if they have a guarantee from an employer that their costs will be covered;
- partnerships with other employers or community groups to foster and develop nursery facilities – where the demand for childcare facilities is small some employers have looked to join with other employers or with local community groups to provide the facilities needed;
- holiday playschemes for older children – childcare needs don't end when children are old enough to go to school, as parents still face the problem of what to do when children are on holiday, or after school. Employers can help in school holidays by providing playschemes on their premises;
- after school care schemes – provision of after school care is sometimes offered by local schools, but where it is not,

employers can help by providing funds to voluntary and community groups to set up and run such schemes or offer schemes on their own premises if appropriate.

Choosing the right childcare package for your organisation

The decision as to what kind of help to provide for childcare will depend on:

- the needs of the staff you employ or the staff that you seem to be losing unnecessarily;
- the size of your organisation;
- the structure of your organisation – whether on one site or split between a number of different sites;
- the working patterns of your employees – regular hours or shift work, weekend work, evening work, etc.;
- the childcare facilities already available in the local area;
- the distances staff travel to work;
- the resources available to you;
- the accommodation available on site.

Identifying demand

You can identify the nature and size of the demand for childcare facilities and obtain information about the kind of help that is likely to be most productive by putting together a statistical profile of your workforce. Ask what proportion of your staff have children and what their ages are. What is the resignation rate of women staff following maternity leave for staff at different levels in the management hierarchy and what proportion of your new recruits are women?

Try interviewing staff who leave your organisation to identify their reasons for resigning. How many might have stayed with the organisation if childcare facilities had been available?

A survey of staff can identify what childcare needs they have and what kind of help would be most effective.

Putting together a business plan

This kind of information can also help you put together a business plan for investment in childcare expenditure (see chapter 11). Any of the above options is likely to involve your company in some expenditure; the most expensive option is a workplace nursery, while the cheapest option is the childminder service, which involves only staff time to research local facilities and to provide advice to parents. They are not necessarily alternatives and you may wish to consider both options. But whatever you decide, you will need to persuade your management that the expenditure is worthwhile. Information about resignation rates and about your staff profile can help you to cost and compare the advantages to your organisation of developing childcare facilities and the disadvantages of failing to do so.

There are a number of benefits to your organisation which can be gained from investment in childcare facilities.

- Reduced staff turnover – use your resignation figures and other relevant information to estimate current staff turnover costs. These include the costs of advertising and recruiting new members of staff, costs of training new staff, loss of investment in training staff who have left, costs of paying for agency staff to cover staff vacancies and lower productivity if vacancies are not filled quickly.
- Reduced absences from work – staff may need to take time away from work to deal with difficulties in providing childcare. The provision of reliable childcare facilities can help to reduce this kind of absence.
- Higher productivity and greater flexibility from staff – the availability of childcare facilities close to work can make it easier for staff to deal with the demands of work as and when they arise and reduce the need to leave work at a fixed time in order to pick up children from childminders etc.
- Improved recruitment – the availability of childcare facilities can be an attraction to potential employees and can enable employers to tap a new section of the labour market. Look at current recruitment patterns to see if your organisation is missing out on recruiting women returners.

Advantages and disadvantages

The childcare needs of your staff and the resources available to you will help determine which of the above options to pursue. Each has advantages and disadvantages and each is appropriate to different circumstances. For example:

Childminder service

ADVANTAGES
Cheap to run and easy to set up; doesn't require any major investment and may be particularly appropriate for small organisations where the

MAKING EQUAL OPPORTUNITIES WORK

demand for childcare facilities is not sufficient to support a workplace nursery.

DISADVANTAGES
The employer has no control over the service and so cannot influence it to meet the needs of its staff.

Childcare vouchers

ADVANTAGES
Easy to set up; allows the organisation to provide support for a large number of employees; provides staff with the opportunity to buy their own childcare at a time and in a place most convenient for them; is a way of providing help for small organisations that could not sustain a workplace nursery, or for organisations where most staff have long journeys to work and do not wish to travel with their children.

DISADVANTAGES
The childcare difficulties that staff face may be as much to do with the availability of childcare facilities as financial difficulties; providing this kind of financial support may therefore be only part of the solution.

Buying places in a nursery

ADVANTAGES
There is no initial capital outlay; provides a solution for small organisations that cannot sustain a nursery; may stimulate the provision of childcare facilities in the community.

DISADVANTAGES
The opening times of the nursery may not be flexible and responsive enough to meet the needs of the organisation.

Partnership nurseries

ADVANTAGES
Shared risk; significant demand for places; particularly appropriate for small organisations.

DISADVANTAGES
The individual employer has less control.

Workplace nursery

ADVANTAGES

Nursery on site and easily accessible for staff; opening times etc. can be matched to the particular needs of the organisation; arrangements for 'day places' for children whose usual childminder is sick etc. can be included in the services provided.

DISADVANTAGES

May be expensive to set up; allows the organisation to help only a limited number of staff.

Playschemes

ADVANTAGES

Cheap and easy to run; can provide facilities for school-age children.

DISADVANTAGES

The main difficulty with holiday playschemes is meeting the demand from staff for places for their children.

After school care

ADVANTAGES

Provides facilities for school age children not generally catered for.

DISADVANTAGES

May be quite difficult to set up; if the scheme operates on site transport from the schools would be required.

Setting up a scheme

NURSERIES

A workplace nursery takes the most detailed planning and will inevitably have a long lead-in time. Here are some of the issues you will need to address.

Identify a suitable site. You will need to consider how much noise will carry to the rest of the building; you will need appropriate toilet, washing and kitchen facilities; you will need accommodation with good natural light; an outdoor play area is also desirable; car parking space will also help.

Check on the regulations in your local authority area for nursery facilities. You will need to seek local authority approval.

Decide on the age ranges you wish to cater for, remembering that the required staff-to-child ratio is higher for under twos than for two to five years olds.

Decide whether you are going to employ the nursery staff yourself or whether you intend to put the operation of the nursery out to tender – there are a number of childcare consultancies who will operate nurseries on behalf of an employer (Try the National Children's Bureau, Under Fives Unit or the Workplace Nurseries Campaign for names and addresses of childcare consultancies – see 'Useful Addresses' section).

If you contract out the operation of the nursery, then the nursery firm has the legal responsibility for running it; if you decide to run the nursery yourself then your company has legal responsibility and you should seek legal advice about, for example, commercial insurance cover for protection against any loss or liability.

Decide what you are going to charge for use of the nursery and how much the subsidy will be – under the tax rules introduced in 1990, such subsidy to staff is likely to be exempt from tax as a benefit in kind, but you should check how the tax rules relate to your particular scheme.

Decide how you are going to publicise the scheme and how you are going to select parents, if demand exceeds places. You might simply opt for a 'first come, first served basis', or you might wish to tie your selection criteria to the recruitment needs of your organisation, giving priority to those parents who are working in an area where recruitment is difficult, or you might wish to take account of special needs, giving priority to single parents for example.

Whatever selection method you use, make sure these are open and publicised and check that the criteria do not unintentionally discriminate against men – childcare facilities must be available to both men and women in the organisation. Use the same approach for checking the effects of your selection criteria as the approach outlined in chapter 3 for checking the effects of selection criteria in recruitment or promotion (The Equal Opportunities Commission will also offer advice – see 'Useful Addresses' section).

Decide what kind of service you will offer. Will you provide lunch for the children or require parents to provide food? What kind of play materials will you need – you may be able to recycle some office materials such as pens, pencils and waste paper for children to use for drawing and painting or for 'papier maché' models. Will there be a quiet room and beds/cots for children to take a nap, and what hours will the nursery be open? A staff survey can help you identify the best kind of service for your organisation.

Make sure you put in place a proper system for registering the children using the nursery, and necessary details about them (see suggestions below for registering children for holiday playschemes).

Monitor the scheme – obtain feedback from parents to ensure that the nursery is meeting their needs.

PLAYSCHEMES

In setting up a holiday playscheme, your first step will also be to identify suitable premises. As the playscheme operates only at certain times of the year, the premises could be rooms in your company premises that can also be used for other functions – access to outdoor space or a nearby park is desirable. The rooms will need to be close to toilet facilities and situated so that noise will not be a problem.

Next, you will need to decide upon the age range – a playscheme will be easier to run if the children are of similar age. You must then decide whether you intend to run the scheme yourself or whether you wish to put the operation of the scheme out to tender; again, you will need to check out the questions of insurance and legal responsibility; if you decide to put the operation of the scheme out to contract much of the detail discussed below will be dealt with by the contractor, but you will need to be satisfied that the arrangements are of a high standard.

Decide how much you are going to charge and how much the employer's subsidy will be – such subsidy is likely to be exempt from tax as a benefit in kind to the employee, but you should check in relation to the particular scheme you are proposing.

Then work out how you are going to publicise the scheme and how you are going to select the parents if demand exceeds the number of places (see comments above on selecting children for a nursery).

Think about the kind of service you want to provide. Do you want to include trips out to museums, zoos etc.; will the children be required to bring their own lunch; what kind of play materials will you need (see table on page 152 for examples of the kind of activities that might be included in a playscheme programme)?

Finally, set up a system for registering the children attending. You should have a simple registration form, which includes:

- child's full name;
- child's age;
- name of parent or other person responsible for delivering and collecting the child and one other emergency contact;

- medical information (allergies etc.);
- name, address and telephone number of child's doctor;
- additional information such as dietary needs, special interests, whether the child can swim etc.

The form should also contain the parent's written consent to the child going on outings and receiving medical attention if necessary in an emergency.

Monitor the scheme – feedback from parents and children will help ensure a good quality service and help you to improve the playscheme to meet the needs of those parents and children who are using it.

Holiday playschemes: activities, visits, toys and equipment
Children aged 5–12

Activities: some examples

Indoor	*Outdoor*	*Outings*
Table tennis	Sports – rounders	Museums
Painting, batik	athletics	Children's theatre
Clay modelling	Treasure Hunts	Sea-side trip
Enamelling, origami	Nature walks	Zoo
Drama	Park swings and	Urban farm
Story telling	roundabouts	Nature reserve
Baking	Swimming	Visit to countryside
Paid entertainment –	Picnic	
puppet show		
magicians		
Quizzes		

Toys and equipment: some examples

Jigsaws
Board games
Art and craft material
Paper, paints, pens, pencils
Balls
Skipping ropes
Cooking equipment
Books
Dressing-up box
Old newspapers for 'papier-mâché'
Cassette recorder
TV and video

OTHER KINDS OF CHILDCARE

For other kinds of help with childcare such as childcare vouchers, advice about local childminders and so on, you will also need to publicise the scheme, decide how much the subsidy to employees will be, check the tax position for your employees and monitor the scheme.

CHECKLIST

A package of flexible working patterns, good parental leave and childcare provision will help your organisation:

- retain staff with domestic responsibilities;
- recruit from a wider section of the labour market;
- reduce staff absences;
- improve morale and performance;
- increase equality of opportunity within your organisation.

The package that is right for your organisation will depend on:

- its size;
- its structure;
- the nature of the work;
- the location.

In setting up new schemes, you will need to:

- identify, through statistical profiles and exit surveys, the main needs and the kind of provisions that might meet these needs;
- make a business case for your senior management;
- consult staff and trade union representatives;
- run a pilot scheme if appropriate;
- publicise the new arrangement within your organisation and in recruitment literature;
- monitor the new arrangements.

CHAPTER 9
Employing People with Disabilities

The principles of good employment practice that have been set out in earlier chapters of this book are an essential starting point for ensuring equality of opportunity for everyone, whatever their sex, race or disability. There are, however, some particular obligations and considerations that you will also need to take account of in ensuring a work environment which is open to people who might have quite severe disabilities. This chapter summarises these obligations, highlights some additional good employment practice and lists some sources of expert help and advice.

Legal obligations

The 1944 Disabled Persons (Employment) Act places certain legal obligations on all employers with 20 or more staff. Under the Act, any person who 'on account of injury, disease or congenital deformity, is substantially handicapped in obtaining or keeping employment, or in undertaking work on his or her own account, of a kind which, apart from that injury, disease or deformity, would be suited to his or her age, experience and qualifications' may register as disabled. Registration is voluntary; it provides the individual with access to certain financial help from the Department of Employment.

Registration also provides a framework for the legal obligations placed on employers. Under the Act, all employers with 20 or more staff are subject to the following obligations. They must employ a minimum of 3% of registered disabled people in their workforce (this is known as the quota scheme). To help achieve this an employer who is below quota can give preference to a person who is registered as disabled when recruiting. An employer who is below the 3% quota is not committing an offence – however, employers who are below quota must not engage anyone other than a registered disabled person without first obtaining a permit to do so from the local jobcentre, or unless they have gained exemption by making an application to the Department of Employment to reduce the quota.

A permit may only be issued to enable employers to fill immediate vacancies or to engage a specified number of workers over a six month period if there are no suitably qualified registered disabled people available. Employers can only make an application to have the quota reduced on the ground that it is too large given the circumstances in which all or any of the persons employed by them are employed.

An employer must not discharge a registered disabled worker without reasonable cause if below quota, or if by discharging the person the employer would become below quota.

An employer employing 20 or more staff must keep records showing the total number and names of all employees as well as the dates they joined the organisation and the date when they leave the organisation. These records must identify registered disabled employees and must be available for inspection by the Department of Employment.

The good practice set out in Chapters 3 and 5 of this book will help you meet the requirements to monitor the number of staff who are registered as disabled and will help you improve your recruitment performance to achieve quota.

The Companies Act 1985 also places certain obligations on employers regarding the employment of people with disabilities generally. The director's report of any company employing on average more than 250 people must contain a statement describing the policy applied during the previous financial year for giving full and fair consideration to people with disabilities applying for jobs, continuing the employment of employees who become disabled whilst working for the company and training, career development and promotion of employees with a disability.

The good practice set out in chapters 4, 5, 6, 7 and 8 of this book will help you meet the requirements of the 1985 Act by ensuring that your recruitment and promotion methods are fair and open and that you can offer the kind of working arrangements that may help staff with more severe disabilities to retain their jobs and perform effectively. The additional good practice set out in this chapter will also help you to ensure that your equal opportunity policies operate effectively.

Finally, as we enter the single european market, you will also need to keep in line with developments in the EEC. The European Commission has already promoted two action programmes for people with disabilities (the Helios programmes) and looks set to launch a third to cover the period 1992–1996. Initiatives to improve employment opportunities for people with disabilities are likely to feature as part of this action programme.

Access and equipment

People with disabilities can often face unnecessary practical problems at work, simply because the work environment does not take account of their needs. The right piece of equipment or the right modification to a building can provide a solution. This may be something quite minor, such as obtaining a magnifying glass, installing a low level light switch or an amplifier for a telephone, or it may be something more extensive, such as the installation of ramps or a lift or the purchase of a braille reader or 'talking' computer. Different individuals will have different needs, and obviously the best people to identify such needs are the individuals themselves. Expert advice is, however, readily available to help find the right solution. There are also some general rules and standards of practice that can help make your organisation and the offices it uses more friendly and accessible for all people with disabilities.

General good practice

Access to buildings

We all experience difficulty in getting round a new and unfamiliar building, but if you have a visual impairment, a mobility problem or even hearing difficulties these problems are compounded. Here are some of the points you should check about your own building to help improve access.

- Is the *entrance* to the building accessible for someone in a wheelchair? Are there ramps as an alternative to any necessary steps into the building? Are the doors wide enough for a wheel chair? Is there an alternative to a revolving door?
- What about *car parking*? Is there parking for people with disabilities close to the entrance of the building?
- Are they any *toilets* for wheelchair users and if so where are they? It's not only important to have toilets available that are suitable for wheelchair users, it's also important that they are easily accessible.
- Are the *doors* to offices wide enough for access in a wheelchair?

- What about access to the *canteen*? Where is the canteen? Does it require going up stairs? Is there a lift available or ramps?
- How do the *lifts* operate? Are the lift buttons low enough to be reached from a wheelchair? What about a voice-synthesiser to announce which floor the lift has stopped at to help people with a visual impairment? What about braille numbers on the lift buttons for people who are blind?
- What about your *emergency alarm system*? Does it rely on a sound alarm or is there also a visual alarm, such as a flashing light?
- Do your *evacuation* procedures take account effectively of the needs of someone with a disability? Do you have any evacuation chairs?
- Are there *maps on the walls and clear signs* in the corridors to indicate where people are? Getting lost is more tiresome and time-consuming for someone with a mobility problem than for others; a good floorplan can help avoid this.

Getting these things right will remove a lot of the practical barriers to employment opportunities for people with disabilities.

There are also some simple guidelines to follow when someone with a disability first joins your organisation:

- invite the individual to visit the building and find their way around before their first day of employment;
- on their first day make sure someone shows them round the building and points out the emergency exits etc.;
- provide a plan of the building showing where any special features (toilets etc.) are located;
- make sure one of the staff with whom they are working takes a special interest and responsibility for the individual for the first few days so that any difficulties that may arise don't go unnoticed and can be easily and quickly dealt with;
- make sure that the manager responsible has access to disability awareness training etc. as appropriate;
- it can be helpful for someone with a disability to have contact with other people in the organisation with a similar disability – check this out and if appropriate foster a mentoring or network system (your trade union may be helpful here);
- check with the individual whether they have any particular needs or requests – the layout and seating arrangements can, for example, be particularly important for someone with a disability – easy access to the doors and corridors can be helpful for someone with a disability, desks need to

be wide enough apart to enable someone in a wheelchair to get around, good lighting is essential for someone with a visual impairment or for someone who relies on lip-reading.

Equipment

Many people with a disability do not need any special equipment to help them perform their job effectively, but some, of course, will. There is a wide range of equipment on the market to help people deal with any problems that may arise. Here are some examples:

VISUAL IMPAIRMENT

- Special computer equipment with, for example, a braille printer to produce written material in braille, or a large print-out device.
- 'Talking' calculators.
- Telephone switchboards with touch indicators or audio output.
- A personal computer/word-processor with a screen that can display enlarged text.
- A portable 'note-taker', which can be used to take notes at a meeting to be printed out later as text or in braille.

Further information can be obtained from the Royal National Institute for the Blind or the Department of Employment Disablement Advisory Service.

HEARING DIFFICULTY

- An amplifier for a telephone.
- An inductive loop system for meetings, conferences etc. which enables speech to be amplified or displayed visually on a screen.

Further information can be obtained from the Royal National Institute for the Deaf and the Department of Employment Disablement Advisory Service.

ARTHRITIS AND RHEUMATISM/DEXTERITY PROBLEMS

- Enlarged telephone keys or a telephone holder.
- Enlarged keyboard for a word processor.
- Page turners.
- Electronic writing systems.

Further information can be obtained from the British Rheumatism and Arthritis Association or the Department of Employment Disablement Advisory Service.

MOBILITY PROBLEM

- Stair-lift.
- Wheelchair lift.
- A 'chair' which can 'climb' stairs and be adjusted to different heights to reach shelves etc.

Further information can be obtained from organisations such as the Spinal Injuries Association or the Department of Employment Disablement Advisory Service.

CHOOSING THE RIGHT EQUIPMENT

The right piece of equipment will depend on the needs of the particular individual and the needs of the particular job. To decide what the right piece of equipment is:

- first consult the individual concerned – he or she will be the best person to identify any difficulties in the job or the surroundings;
- if necessary seek expert advice – the Department of Employment's Disablement Advisory Service will provide advice free of charge;
- take up opportunities to visit exhibitions of equipment; encourage staff with difficulties to do the same. There is an annual exhibition of equipment organised by NADEX which takes place in London and in other major cities (for more information, contact the Royal Association for Disability and Rehabilitation, address on page 164 below). Organisations such as the Disabled Living Foundation are also happy to allow visitors to try out equipment.

If your organisation is large enough, you may consider setting up your own exhibition of equipment. An exhibition of this kind can be helpful in a number of ways:

- staff with disabilities can try out equipment, see how it works and learn about the availability of new equipment;
- managers of staff with disabilities and personnel managers can gain a better understanding of the way in which special equipment can help people with disabilities improve their performance;
- staff and managers will be able to see people with

disabilities using the equipment and will gain a better understanding both of the kind of problems that people with disabilities can face at work and the way in which these can be overcome. This can be helpful in raising awareness generally and giving a high profile to your company's disability employment policies.

It need not be difficult or expensive to run. You simply need a space big enough to display the equipment – a couple of large conference rooms or a sports hall, for example. The rooms that you use will need plenty of power points, good lighting, tables for displaying the equipment and access for people with disabilities. Manufacturers will usually be happy to come and display their equipment free of charge (though you should be prepared to provide refreshments for them during the exhibition) and the Department of Employment's Disablement Advisory Service should be able to provide information about their names and addresses.

A commitment to good employment practice

The Department of Employment launched a new initiative in 1990 to encourage the spread of good practice in the employment of people with disabilities. Employers are encouraged to use a new symbol to demonstrate their commitment to good policies and practices in employing people with disabilities. The symbol can be used in company literature and in recruitment advertising, and its use is likely to help improve your recruitment performance by giving a positive message to potential recruits who may have a disability, and encouraging applications from them. To be effective, of course, the symbol needs to be backed up by an effective equal opportunity policy so that the positive message that is conveyed is in fact delivered. The Department of Employment's Disablement Advisory Service can give you more information about this symbol and about other schemes described in the following paragraphs.

Sources of help and advice

The main source of help and advice about the employment of people with disabilities is the Department of Employment. Financial support is also available through the Department of Employment. There are, in addition, also a number of individual voluntary organisations – some with specialist knowledge of particular disabilities and others with particular expertise in employment issues – who will be willing to provide advice.

Department of employment

The Department of Employment operates three main employment services for people with disabilities and employers. These are the disablement resettlement officer (DRO) service, the disablement advisory service (DAS) and the employment rehabilitation service (ERS). You can find out more about each of these services from your local job centre.

Disablement resettlement officers essentially help people with a disability find a job. They deal with training and placing in employment any person with a disability. They can help employers find suitable job applicants and if you have a vacancy in your organisation you should inform the DRO at your local job centre.

The Disablement Resettlement Officer service can also give advice about the Job Introduction scheme. This is a scheme that provides financial support to an employer for a trial period when a disabled employee is first recruited and the employer has reservations about whether the employee is able to do the job, or when an existing employee becomes disabled and the employer is uncertain whether or not the employee will be able to continue to carry out his or her job if retained.

The disablement advisory service provides a service to employers on all aspects of the employment of people with disabilities and particularly on adaptations to premises and equipment. There are more than 70 DAS teams cover all parts of the UK. DAS teams will help any employer in the development of their equal opportunity policies for people with disabilities and will also give advice about any particular needs or difficulties of individual employees or job applicants. DAS also operates and can give advice about the various special schemes that are operated by the Department of Employment. For example:

- adaptation to premises and equipment scheme – a scheme through which employers can obtain grants towards the adaptation of premises to accommodate a particular member of staff with a disability, or towards special equipment;
- fares to work scheme – financial assistance to help a person with a disability overcome difficulties travelling to work – a grant of up to 75% of the cost of fares is available to people whose disability is so severe as to prevent them from using public transport to get to work;
- financial and practical assistance to enable an employer to take on a disabled trainee – if an employer provides training places in the Department of Employment's programme for unemployed adults there is a range of help

available to accommodate disabled trainees (information from your local Training and Enterprise Council);

- sheltered placement scheme – described in more detail in chapter 8 – financial assistance is available to help provide new employment opportunities for people with particularly severe disabilities, and to help employers retain staff who become severely disabled;
- remote working scheme – described in more detail in chapter 8 – financial assistance is available to help provide home-working opportunities for people whose disability prevents travel to work.

The employment rehabilitation service provides a service for both employers and people with disabilities, and can be particularly helpful where an existing member of staff becomes disabled. The ERS have a number of assessment and training centres. They will carry out employment assessments for people with disabilities, providing advice on the most suitable types of work and on any necessary equipment.

Voluntary organisations

There are many different voluntary organisations with expertise in the employment of people with disabilities. Some are national organisations and some local. The Council for Voluntary Organisations in your town, your local authority or the library service should be able to provide you with a list of useful contacts in the locality of your company, but here is a list of national organisations that you may also find helpful.

British Epilepsy Association
Anstey House
40 Hanover Square
Leeds
LS3 1BE

British Rheumatism and Arthritis Association
5 Grosvenor Crescent
London
SW1X 7ER

Disabled Living Foundation
380–384 Harrow Road
London
W9 2HY
For information and advice about equipment to help people at work.

Link Employment
54 Blyth Road
London
W14 OHA
For advice and information about mental health problems at work.

Multiple Sclerosis Society
25 Essie Road
Fulham
London
SW6 1EE

Royal Association for Disability and Rehabilitation
25 Mortimer Street
London
W1N 8AB

Royal National Institute for the Blind
224 Great Portland Street
London
W1N 6AA
Has a national employment service. In particular, RNIB runs the *Personal Reader Service* in England and Wales (in Scotland this service is run by the Disablement Advisory Service). If an employer wishes to recruit a blind or partially-sighted person, or to retain the services of an employee who becomes blind or partially sighted, financial assistance is available to enable that person to engage a part-time reader.

Royal National Institute for the Deaf
105 Gower Street
London
WC1E 6AH
Operates an employment service.

Royal Society for Mentally Handicapped Children and Adults (MENCAP)
Pathway Employment Service
169a City Road
Cardiff
CF2 3JB
The Pathway Employment Service operates a scheme to encourage the employment of people with a mental handicap. Under the scheme an employer can obtain financial help during a trial or training period for a worker with a mental disability.

The Spastics Society
12 Park Crescent
London
W1N 3EQ

The Spinal Injuries Association
Yeoman's House
St James' Lane
London
N10 3DF

As a group, people with disabilities have the same range of skills, knowledge and abilities as other employees. With good planning, appropriately planned accommodation and access to any necessary equipment there are few – if any – jobs that suitably qualified people with even the severest disabilities are unable to carry out effectively and efficiently. Providing access to equipment and ensuring that there are no practical barriers in the layout or physical design of the building is an important equal opportunity issue for people with disabilities.

There is a wide range of expertise and advice outlined in this chapter that employers can call upon, as well as financial help and support. Following the general good equal opportunity practice set out in the earlier chapters in this book, and the additional good practice set out in this chapter, will help ensure that your employer can meet the obligations under the Disabled Persons (Employment) Act 1944 and the Companies Act, 1985.

CHAPTER 10
The Working Environment

However effective your equal opportunity policy is, complaints of perceived or actual discrimination are still likely to arise. The very fact that a company has an equal opportunity policy may make this more likely. Behaviour that went unreported before will be drawn to the attention of management as standards of good practice are set. It is, therefore, important to establish a positive environment in which such complaints can be made and dealt with in an open and constructive manner. An environment in which such complaints are discouraged, quickly dismissed or ignored, or in which the complainant is victimised or criticised for 'causing trouble' will undermine the company's equal opportunity policies, call into question the credibility of such policies and may lead to costly industrial tribunal cases.

The working environment itself can also undermine your equal opportunity policies and present barriers to equality in other ways. The behaviour of male staff towards women and of white staff towards black and Asian staff can either help or hinder the effectiveness of an organisation's equal opportunity policies. A hostile environment in which racist and sexist remarks go unchallenged and in which harassment is allowed to occur can undermine those staff towards whom such behaviour is directed, and can lower morale, lower productivity, cause unnecessary stress and in some cases ill-health. A positive environment in which women and ethnic minorities are welcomed and valued will, on the other hand, help to ensure that all staff have the full opportunity to work effectively and develop their full potential.

This chapter looks first at how to deal with complaints of discrimination, and secondly at sexual and racial harassment and what employers can do to minimise such behaviour.

Dealing with complaints of discrimination

Many employers act defensively when faced with a complaint of discrimination. They close ranks behind the manager accused, and go to great lengths to find evidence to support and justify his or her actions. Many actually prefer to admit incompetence rather than concede that they have practiced race or sex discrimination, even where the complaint is one of indirect discrimination and there is no question of a discriminatory motive to explain the different effects of the procedure. Failing to deal effectively with complaints of discrimination will undermine the effectiveness of the company's equal opportunity policy. It may mean the loss of able and competent staff who choose to leave the organisation as a result of discriminatory practice, and may also lead to the company's involvement in industrial tribunal cases.

Fighting an industrial tribunal case brings with it many disadvantages:

- It is expensive and time-consuming;
- It is hurtful to all concerned. The reasons for decisions, actions or failures to act, are examined in detail, in public. Tribunals comment critically on mistakes, and failures to carry out policy and incompetence.
- There may be damaging publicity.
- Your company will be seen to be putting its resources into fighting a discrimination charge. This will publicly undermine your claims to be an equal opportunity employer and may make recruitment more difficult.
- It is very difficult to restore normal working relationships after cases have been fought.
- Energy is devoted to defence, and to justifying actions taken. This makes it more difficult for managers to stand back and consider the lessons; and ask 'could we have acted better?'.

The complaints procedure

These disadvantages amount to a strong case for trying to settle and resolve complaints effectively within the organisation and at an early stage, wherever possible. To achieve this, you will need an effective complaints procedure. It is neither necessary nor desirable for this procedure to be separate from the company's normal grievance procedure. Complaints of discrimination can, however, raise sensitive and difficult issues. It is therefore important to ensure that your complaints procedure can deal effectively with the particular circumstances and characteristics of complaints of race or sex discrimination and that the complaints procedure is well publicised.

You should publish, in the context of the company's equal opportunity policy statement, a statement which makes it clear that employees have the right to complain about discrimination and explains to them how to go about this.

Tell employees that they may be represented by their shop steward or an employee of their choice. The latter may be particularly important in the case of sexual harassment where a female victim may prefer to be represented by a woman. Offer, where possible, interpreting facilities to complainants with language difficulties.

Allow for an initial informal approach, which is not recorded in a complainant's personal file unless he or she wishes to pursue the matter further. This is likely to encourage early action on the part of the victim so that appropriate steps can be taken to deal with the situation and prevent it becoming more serious or difficult to resolve. Many problems can be solved informally to the satisfaction of all those involved if action is taken at an early stage. The opportunity to raise such matters informally with someone other than a line manager – for example, a personnel manager, the equal opportunity adviser or other person – is important (particularly in the case of sexual harassment).

If the complaint cannot be resolved informally, the next step is to ensure that the complaint is formally investigated in an open and positive manner and, if possible, by someone independent of the department to which the complaint relates, and by someone who knows how discrimination at work can occur. This will help inspire confidence in all those involved in the fairness and impartiality of the complaints process. You should also make sure that both the complainant and the person complained against know their rights, that complaints are dealt with quickly and that the outcome of grievance procedures are communicated to those involved.

Review complaints so that any general lessons which emerge can be fed back into the policy process and acted upon if necessary.

If you are faced with a complaint you will need to decide whether the complaint is valid, and if so what steps to take. To help make this judgement in a complaint about recruitment or promotion procedures, for example, you will need to make the following enquiries:

- establish the relevant facts about the complainant, for example ethnic origin, sex, age, qualifications, seniority date, date of application, interview, previous work experience and conduct;

- establish how the complainant was treated, when and by whom, and the reason for any decisions;
- list the same data for all other comparable applicants or employees in the job or promotion complained about;
- look for differences in treatment and the reasons;
- check whether there is a discriminatory pattern in the decisions;
- check against any other formal criteria and practices;
- check whether your equal opportunity policy has been followed.

Warning signs

- Disproportionate rejection of women or ethnic minorities at any stage of your selection/assessment procedure.
- Criteria or procedures not followed or inconsistently applied.
- Vague or subjective reasons for decisions.
- Selectors not trained.
- Selectors and managers unaware of equal opportunity policy.
- Equal opportunity policy not applied on documents.
- Racial or sexual comments/abuse and derogatory language.
- Complainant treated unfairly, or complaints ignored or belittled.

If any of these warning signs are present, you should recognise that discrimination may have taken place and consider redressing the complaintant's grievance and putting your practices right. The presence of any of these factors would put you in difficulty if the case came before an industrial tribunal.

Here are some of the actions you may need to take:

- compensate the victim for loss of opportunity and for hurt feelings;
- apologise;
- consider offering the victim a transfer to alternative work (if desired – do not try to impose a change of job), or promotion or training;
- if you decide the complainant's case is justified, disciplinary action and/or counselling and/or training of the member of staff complained of;
- re-affirm or revise your equal opportunity policy and review the offending practice or criteria;
- improve monitoring and establish targets for improving any under-representation.

Finally, if all else fails and you have to fight an industrial tribunal case, make sure that you have made some tangible improvements, such as those listed above, that you can offer the tribunal and that you have done all you can to investigate the case and resolve it properly. This will be evidence of your good faith in making your equal opportunity policy effective. If you do have to fight an industrial tribunal case also remember that follow-up action in the form of counselling and support for those involved in the case will be particularly important.

Establishing an effective complaints procedure is a key element of any equal opportunity programme. It is essential that staff feel able to make their grievances known and confident that their concerns will be treated seriously. Complaints of discrimination are not necessarily an indication of a failure of the company's equal opportunity policies. They may simply reflect the fact that staff recognise that fair and equal treatment is firmly on the company agenda. Failure to deal with complaints of discrimination will undermine the effectiveness of the company's equal opportunity policy, may lead to a high turnover rate among women and ethnic minorities, and may lead to costly industrial tribunal cases. Complaints of discrimination are not, however, just bad news for the company. They can indicate where policies and practices are going wrong and how they can be put right.

Further guidance or grievance procedures is available in a guide produced by the Commission for Racial Equality, *Racial Discrimination and Grievance Procedures*.

Sexual and racial harassment

What is harassment?

Racial harassment can be a form of racial discrimination. It is not, however, concerned with practices and procedures, rather it is concerned with the individual behaviour of one person towards another. It may involve:

- racist insults and ridicule;
- the use of racist names (e.g. 'coon', 'wog', 'nigger');
- racist jokes;
- display of racist literature;
- threatening behaviour intended to persuade the individual to leave the company, or in its worst form
- assault (this would, of course, also be a criminal offence).

Sexual harassment can similarly be sex discrimination arising from the behaviour of individuals. Both men and women can be the victims of sexual harassment. In practice, however, it is a form of behaviour which almost always involves a man as the perpetrator and a woman as the victim. It is a very particular form of sex discrimination. Some sex discrimination derives from sexual stereotypes such as 'women being good cooks and poor engineers', 'women being emotional and unable to cope with pressure' or 'women being non-assertive'. Sex discrimination in the form of sexual harassment focuses on women's sexuality. It covers a wide range of behaviours. The essential characteristics of sexual harassment are that the behaviour is of a sexual nature, unreciprocated and unwelcome, deliberate and persistent.

TUC guidelines (1982) define sexual harassment as including:

repeated and unwanted verbal or sexual advances, sexually explicit derogatory statements or sexually discriminating remarks which are offensive to the worker involved, which cause the worker to feel threatened, humiliated, patronised or harassed or which interfere with the worker's job performance, undermine job security or create a threatening or intimidating work environment.

In the US, the Equal Employment Opportunity Commission have defined sexual harassment as:

unwelcome sexual behaviour that makes submission a condition of decisions affecting an individual's employment or that creates a hostile or offensive working environment.

The EC has provided a definition of sexual harassment. In 1990, the EC Council of Ministers enacted a resolution on the protection of the dignity of women and men at work. The resolution provided for the first time an official definition of sexual harassment and set a standard for action which, although not legally binding, applies throughout the Member States. Sexual harassment is defined in the EC Council resolution as

conduct of a sexual nature, or other conduct based on sex affecting the dignity of women and men at work, including conduct of superiors and colleagues, if
(a) such conduct is unwanted, unreasonable and offensive to the recipient;
(b) a person's rejection of or submission to such conduct ... is used explicitly or implicitly as a basis for a decision which affects that person's access to vocational training, access to employment,

continued employment, promotion, salary or any other employment decisions; and/or

(c) such conduct creates an intimidating, hostile or humiliating work environment for the recipient.

This definition stems from an earlier EC report concerning sexual harassment at work (Michael Rubenstein, *The Dignity of Women at Work*).

The kind of unwanted behaviour that can be involved in sexual harassment includes:

- letters, telephone calls or material of a sexual nature;
- leering, jokes, ridicule, unwelcome comments about dress or appearance, embarrassing sexual remarks, sexual teasing;
- verbal abuse and name-calling;
- deliberate touching, leaning over or pinching;
- sexually suggestive looks or gestures;
- uninvited pressure for sexual favours;
- pressure for dates;
- sexual assault.

How often does harassment occur?

Sexual and racial harassment occurs more often than is generally supposed and much of it goes unreported. Staff may choose to tolerate such harassment rather than draw attention to themselves by reporting it, or they may take their own action to end or avoid harassment simply by leaving the organisation. Though harassment appears to be more likely to occur in certain working environments than in others – for example in situations in which women or ethnic minorities are represented in only very small numbers (perhaps one woman working with a group of male colleagues), and in situations in which women and ethnic minorities are exclusively in the lowest grade jobs, it is clear that harassment can and does occur across a wide range of organisations and working environments.

If we look at survey evidence about the incidence of sexual harassment, for example, we find that the majority of women claim to experience some form of harassment during their career. In January 1982 the Alfred Marks Bureau undertook a survey of 799 employees and managers who used their agency. More than 60% of employees reported that they had experienced sexual harassment at work on at least one occasion. Similar results have emerged from surveys undertaken by NALGO of local government employees, and surveys of women managers demonstrate that harassment is not confined to women at the more junior levels (see *Women and Harassment at Work* by Nathalie Hadjifotiou, Pluto Press, 1983).

Is sexual and racial harassment against UK law?

UK law provides no definition of either racial or sexual harassment. Despite the absence of a specific legal definition of harassment, such forms of behaviour have, nevertheless, been found to constitute direct sex or race discrimination. In Chapter 12 we provide some examples of industrial tribunal cases concerning incidents of racial and sexual harassment. The fact that harassment can constitute race or sex discrimination means that an employer is responsible for taking steps to ensure that employees do not practise sexual or racial harassment, just as an employer is legally responsible for other acts of discrimination by an employee.

What action can an employer take to prevent harassment at work?

The first and most important step that an employer can take to prevent harassment at work is to recognise that harassment at work can and does happen. The second is to recognise that the employer has a responsibility to take action to help prevent such harassment occurring. Both the Commission for Racial Equality and Equal Opportunity Commission codes of practice on employment identify the prevention of harassment as good employment practice. The EC Council resolution on sexual harassment also makes this clear. The resolution calls on Member States to:

remind employers that they have a responsibility to seek to ensure that the work environment is free from:
(a) unwanted conduct of a sexual nature or other conduct based on sex affecting the dignity of women and men at work; and
(b) victimisation of a complainant or of a person wishing to give, or giving, evidence in the event of a complaint.

Here are some of the steps that employers can take to help prevent harassment occurring and to ensure that when it does occur it is dealt with effectively:

- adopt and publicise a policy statement;
- establish an effective complaints procedure;
- ensure that any necessary follow-up action is taken when harassment occurs;
- monitor and review complaints;
- provide training for managers and staff.

Policy statements

Publicising policy statements on racial and sexual harassment is an essential starting point for:

- increasing awareness and understanding of the nature of harassment;
- setting standards of acceptable behaviour;
- encouraging employees who are victims of harassment to tell their manager or personnel manager; and
- encouraging managers to take action to establish a working environment free from harassment.

The issues that you will need to cover in a policy statement of this kind are:

- a statement that harassment and related behaviour, such as the display of photographs of naked women, will not be tolerated;
- an explanation of the kind of behaviour that can constitute harassment;
- an explanation of the damage that harassment can cause both for the individual and for the organisation as a whole;
- an explanation of the legal position regarding harassment; and
- an explanation of the complaints procedure.

Complaints procedure

The good practice already outlined at the beginning of this chapter for dealing with complaints of race and sex discrimination applies equally to complaints of racial and sexual harassment. There are, however, other special considerations in cases of harassment. The prime and most pressing concern of staff who are victims of harassment will be to stop the harassment. It is therefore particularly important that staff should know how to make a complaint and staff should have the opportunity to resolve problems of harassment informally.

Some members of staff may be put off reporting harassment if they think that they will inevitably become involved in a lengthy and formal complaints procedure. They will not want to draw attention to themselves; they may fear that the complaint will not be taken seriously because it is their word against the word of someone more senior; or they may be unwilling to involve the harasser in formal disciplinary procedures. The possibility of a formal complaint should always be available to any victim of harassment, and in some cases the employer may decide that this is necessary whatever the views of the victim, but the option of informal action will help ensure that harassment is reported and resolved at an early stage.

Staff should have the opportunity to make a complaint outside the line management system. Where the usual procedure is to make a complaint in the first instance to a line manager or personnel manager, make sure that alternative procedures are available for cases of harassment. It is possible that the line manager may be the harasser or party to the harassment. In such cases a personnel manager may be the right person to deal with a complaint. However, a woman may find it easier to make a complaint of sexual harassment to another woman. You should therefore make sure that women 'contact officers' are available as a first point of call for victims of sexual harassment. A contact officer of this sort can provide support to a victim who wishes to confront the harasser to try and resolve the situation informally, can ensure that the victim knows what options are open to her for making a complaint and can provide support and represent the victim during any formal grievance procedure.

If a formal complaint is made you will need to investigate this carefully and sensitively. Statistical information of the kind that may help you to identify whether or not discrimination has occurred in promotion will not be available. You will need to rely on interviews with all those involved, any documentary evidence in the form, for example, of notes written to the victim or other warning signs in the behaviour of either the complainant or the person complained about. Such warning signs may include:

- a sudden increase in the amount of sick leave taken by the complainant – an indication of stress;
- difficult or emotional behaviour by the complainant – again an indication of stress;
- a pattern of unwanted trips away from the office or late night working being required of the complainant by the person complained of;
- a pattern of the person complained of taking a sudden detailed and unwelcome interest in the victim's work etc.;
- where the harassment is by a group of colleagues, the victim being isolated and excluded from social activities at lunchtime etc.

TAKING NECESSARY FOLLOW-UP ACTION

Where harassment occurs it will be particularly important to ensure that the right follow-up action is taken. It may be necessary to do more than simply stop the behaviour and deal with the individual responsible for the harassment. You should consider what can be done to prevent harassment occurring again. It may be helpful to:

- provide counselling and support for the victim of harassment;
- discuss with those working with the victim of harassment or working with the harasser what they might have done to help prevent the situation occurring;
- provide counselling for the harasser – many men are not aware of how their own behaviour can intimidate and offend women staff, and counselling can help someone who is guilty of harassment to recognise what is wrong about their behaviour and can prevent it happening again;
- monitor and review the way in which the complaint was dealt with to identify any lessons which can help improve your company's policies and procedures in the future.

Monitoring

Monitoring complaints of harassment and the way in which the complaints procedure operates is as important as monitoring any other aspect of your equal opportunity policy. It will help you identify where and in what kind of circumstances harassment occurs and how the complaints procedure can be improved. It will also tell you something about the frequency with which harassment occurs. However, you should remember that an increase in the number of harassment cases reported may simply reflect the fact that your organisation now has an established and successful policy and complaints procedure, rather than any actual increase in the incidence of harassment. Reviewing the way in which a particular case of harassment was dealt with will also help you to understand the way in which your policies are working and help you to further improve it. Here are some of the questions you should ask.

- Was action taken as soon as the incident was brought to the attention of management?
- How effective was this action in meeting the immediate needs of the victim, in preventing the continuation of harassment or in dealing with the harasser?
- How effective was the action in meeting the longer term needs of the victim, the harasser and others involved? Finding the victim a different job may, for example, solve the immediate problem but in the longer term may make the victim feel the one who is to blame.
- Could any steps have been taken to avoid such harassment

occurring? Has the perpetrator(s) of the harassment been involved in such behaviour before? Did other members of staff know about the harassment and if so could they/did they do anything about it? Was this the first time a woman/ethnic minority had worked in this part of the organisation and if so what steps were taken/could have been taken to ensure a positive environment?

- Was the victim/harasser fully aware of the company's equal opportunity policy?

Training

Harassment can often occur because staff do not understand or recognise such behaviour and may continue because managers do not feel competent to deal with the situation. Men, for example, may regard jokes and sexual teasing simply as good fun. The same can be the case when racist jokes are made; black staff who object to such jokes may simply be seen as having no sense of humour or 'having a chip on their shoulder'. Effective staff training will help support your policies for preventing harassment at work by providing:

- an understanding of what harassment is, how it can arise and what the effects can be on the victim;
- an understanding of why it is important to an employer to prevent such behaviour, what the costs are and what the legal implications are;
- the confidence and skills to deal with harassment as a personnel officer, manager, colleague or victim; and
- an understanding of the complaints procedure and the role of individuals in that procedure.

Like other equal opportunity training, this is best achieved by building sessions concerning harassment into existing training courses for staff and managers.

Once you have recognised this your organisation can do a good deal to prevent it by

- publicising a policy statement;
- setting up an effective complaints procedure;
- ensuring effective follow-up action is taken to any complaint;
- monitoring and reviewing complaints;
- ensuring staff training deals with matters of harassment and discrimination.

CHAPTER 11
Costs and Benefits

Implementing an equal opportunity programme will require both staff and financial resources. The resources required will depend on the size of the organisation and the nature of the equal opportunity programme you are implementing. But there are also financial benefits for the organisation. A clear plan of action and an analysis of the financial costs and benefits of your proposed programme will help you to compete effectively for resources within your organisation. The ideas and examples of good practice given in the preceding chapters of this book are intended to help you to develop an effective equal opportunities action plan for your organisation. This chapter is intended to help you to work out the costs of such a programme and to measure the financial benefits that may accrue.

Costs

The costs of your equal opportunity programme fall into two main categories: running costs and capital costs.

Running costs

STAFF COSTS

First there are direct staff costs, for example the salaries of equal opportunity staff, equal opportunity trainers and staff to operate a workplace nursery.

In some cases, it may be sensible and cheaper to buy in consultants rather than recruiting and appointing your own staff. There are, for example, an increasing number of equal opportunity trainers, consultants who will undertake an audit of your organisation and help you develop an action plan, and agencies who will analyse your childcare needs and set up and run childcare facilities.

There are other staff costs which may arise from staff time taken in attending equal opportunity training. Other similar costs may arise from time spent in other activities such as outreach work, participation in discussion groups etc.

OTHER COSTS

Recruitment initiatives might include the costs of extra advertising in the ethnic minority press, the disability press etc., and computer time involved in monitoring recruitment applications.

Promotion initiatives might include the costs of computer time involved in monitoring the promotion process.

Costs of communicating the policy might include the costs of preparing an equal opportunities newsletter, publicising an equal opportunity policy statement and preparing an annual report of progress.

Training costs might include the preparation, development or purchase of training material and other consumables used in training courses.

Childcare initiatives might include the costs of provision of toys and other play material; costs of surveying staff childcare needs and publicising the availability of childcare provision; catering and laundry costs; insurance costs etc. (many of the costs are, however, recoverable from charges to parents).

The costs of a career break scheme might include the costs of producing a newsletter to keep in touch with those on a career break; the costs of occasional seminars for those on career breaks; costs of advertising part-time working and home working opportunities in the organisation and the costs of maintaining a register of those looking for such opportunities.

Capital costs

Monitoring costs might include the purchase of computer software to be used to undertake the necessary analyses.

Childcare costs might involve the purchase of property to use as a nursery, conversion costs, the purchase of necessary furniture and equipment.

Costs to improve the work environment for people with a disability might include the costs of purchasing special equipment or the costs of installing ramps etc. (grants towards such costs are available – see Chapter 9).

Costs of setting up flexible working pattern might include the purchase of computer equipment to monitor a flexible working hours system, and the purchase of any additional necessary equipment to enable staff to work from home effectively.

In presenting those costs to your senior management it is important to evaluate them in relation to their likely present and future benefits. You need to think about the following questions:

- What is the cost of your equal opportunity programme per head of staff?
- How is the cost discounted over time?
- If you are investing in a new piece of equipment such as a new computer system for monitoring purposes, what are the other benefits to the organisation? How can the spare capacity be used to good effect within your organisation?
- If you are providing new facilities such as a workplace nursery, how many staff will the facility directly benefit?
- What are the wider financial benefits to your organisation?

Benefits

A good equal opportunity policy means a more effective recruitment and personnel management policy. A more effective recruitment and personnel management policy can make your organisation more competitive, more productive and more cost effective. Some of the financial benefits that can accrue are set out below:

The ability to recruit from a wider section of the labour market

This will help ensure that vacancies are filled quickly and that your company recruits the best people for the jobs available. You can calculate the financial benefit to your organisation by looking at:

- *vacancy rates:* how long does it take to fill vacancies and what is the average recruitment cost per vacancy filled?
- *recruitment success:* how satisfactory is the quality of the staff recruited, how long do they stay, how many fail to meet the required standards?
- *vacancy costs:* how are staff vacancies covered and what are the costs – overtime costs, costs of agency staff etc.?

The ability to retain staff

Especially those who might otherwise leave for domestic reasons or because they can see no future for 'people like themselves' in the organisation. This will help minimise your recruitment costs and maximise the investment in staff training and development. You can calculate the financial benefit to your organisation by calculating how much you might save on:

- *recruiting new staff:* advertising costs, staff time in processing application forms and arranging interviews, staff time in carrying out interviews;
- *training new staff:* most new staff will need an initial 'training' period and in some cases this may be quite lengthy and involve formal training courses or apprenticeships, in other cases it may simply be on-the-job training over an initial settling-in period, but whatever kind of training is needed there are costs involved, both of staff time and of fees etc. for attending training courses;
- *losing the skills and abilities of staff:* organisations can invest a good deal of time and money in training and developing staff, and the benefits from this investment will only be partially fulfilled if staff leave the organisation early in their career.

Improved staff morale

Good staff morale will also improve retention rates and will help achieve a high level of productivity and commitment to the organisation. Possible financial benefits of good morale include saving the cost of the effects of resignations and fewer costly industrial tribunals. Also a good morale means a good image – it may be difficult to recruit staff to a company with a poor reputation.

Improved service delivery and client satisfaction

An organisation whose workforce reflects the make-up of the client group it is serving and whose workforce responds positively to clients and potential clients, whatever their race, sex or background is likely to have better client relationships.

Value for money

An equal opportunity programme can offer value for money for your organisation. Costing the different elements of your equal opportunity programme and evaluating these against the savings that are likely to accrue will be helpful in the following ways.

First, in planning your programme. It will help you decide on your priorities and will help you decide between different kinds of intervention. For example, there are a number of different ways in which an organisation can help with childcare arrangements – a workplace nursery, purchase of places in an existing convenient nursery, childcare vouchers, help in finding childminders. Each of these methods of invervention can help retain staff and avoid the costs of recruiting and training new staff, but each has different costs associated with it and each has the potential for benefiting different numbers of staff, or staff with different needs. Assessing the financial costs and benefits of each method of intervention can help you decide on the right approach for your organisation.

Secondly, in ensuring that adequate resources are available. You will need to compete for resources within your organisation. So a well-planned and documented equal opportunity 'business plan' will help you to secure adequate resources for your equal opportunity programme.

Thirdly, in obtaining the support and commitment of senior management, the board of directors and shareholders. If you are able to demonstrate the *potential* value for money of your equal opportunity programme and, through monitoring progress, the *actual* value for money of the programme, you are more likely to secure and retain the support of senior managers, directors and shareholders.

Finally, in engendering realistic expectations. An equal opportunity programme is unlikely to bring overnight success. The success of a new initiative may be easier to demonstrate in some cases than in others.

For example, the introduction of part-time working is highly visible and has clear objectives and is targeted at a clearly defined group – women with childcare responsibilities, particularly those returning from maternity leave. Experience suggests that the introduction of part-time working is likely to be popular and by monitoring resignation rates and the number of part-time working opportunities created, you can demonstrate and cost the benefits to the organisation. Other forms of intervention may have longer term benefits, or the benefits may be more difficult to isolate and measure. For example, advertising in the ethnic minority press is unlikely to produce a sudden and dramatic increase in the number of black and Asian people applying to work in your organisation; the benefits are likely to be more long term as the image of the organisation changes and the confidence of the ethnic minority community in the goodwill of that organisation increases. A clear view of the objectives, their likely benefits and the costs will help achieve realistic expectations.

CHAPTER 12
Discrimination Law in Practice

In this chapter we look at some key decisions in race and sex discrimination cases which contain useful lessons for managers. It is not intended as a comprehensive guide to discrimination law, but gives examples which illustrate how the law underpins the need for you to practice equality of opportunity. The cases cover some common mistakes and explain how to avoid making such mistakes. Finally, we include advice on what to do if you are faced with an application to an industrial tribunal.

How do industrial tribunals decide what is discriminatory?

The applicant (person making a complaint) has to show, on the balance of probabilities, that he or she has suffered race or sex discrimination. Tribunals have, however, recognised that overt statements of discriminatory reasoning are rare. That is to say, few people will say openly that they refused to employ someone because he or she is black, or a woman, although occasionally people will admit to discrimination because of someone else's prejudices: 'I cannot appoint a woman to this job because my clients will not accept her.'

Two legal decisions illustrate how tribunals may draw inferences about race and sex discrimination where no one has explicitly admitted to a discriminatory reason. In *Khanna* v. *Ministry of Defence* ([1981] IRLR 331, EAT), the Employment Appeal Tribunal said that where there was nothing available to indicate a discriminatory reason, the tribunal should draw an inference from the facts. If there has been less favourable treatment of an applicant compared with others, the employer must give an explanation for the difference in treatment. If there is no clear and specific explanation, the tribunal may infer that there was a race or sex discrimination.

This reasoning was repeated in *Chattopadhyay* v. *Headmaster of*

Holloway School [1982]. Here the Employment Appeal Tribunal ruled that an employer must satisfy a tribunal that there is an innocent explanation for a complainant being treated less favourably. Tribunals are increasingly looking beyond the circumstances of the individual complaint for an explanation. In particular they will look at evidence which indicates a pattern of decisions against women or ethnic minority people (for example, see *West Midlands PTE* v. *Singh* [1989].

Tribunals take a similar approach in considering whether there has been indirect discrimination. In *Jones* v. *Chief Adjudication Officer* [1991], the Court of Appeal set out useful guidelines:

1. Identify the criteria for selection.
2. Identify the relevant population, comprising all those who satisfy all the other criteria for selection.
3. Divide the relevant population into groups representing those who satisfy the criterion and those who do not.
4. Predict statistically what proportion of each group should be women.
5. Ascertain what are the actual male/female balances of the two groups.
6. Compare the actual with the predicted balances.
7. If women are found to be under-represented in the first group and over-represented in the second, it is proved that the criterion is discriminatory.

You would then have to justify the discriminatory criterion; for example show that it is closely related to job performance.

Ask the following questions if you are faced with a claim of discrimination.

- Has the complainant been treated less favourably? Why were others refused a job or promotion? Was anyone else refused in the same circumstances? Did you apply the rules evenly?
- Does the difference in treatment call for an explanation? Was there inconsistency? Arbitrariness? Personal bias? Were the selection criteria followed? (See Chapter 5 for examples of discriminatory decisions.)
- Is there a pattern of decisions against women or ethnic minorities? How can these other decisions be explained?

Race and Sex Discrimination Law at Work

The Sex Discrimination and Race Relations Acts have almost identical provisions in relation to work. These make it unlawful to discriminate in employment, and contracts for employment with the self-employed in:

(a) the arrangements made for determining who shall be offered employment, that is, recruitment and selection;

(b) the terms of employment and access to benefits and facilities (but the equivalent terms for men and women are covered by the Equal Pay Act 1970);

(c) refusing or deliberately omitting to offer employment;

(d) access to opportunities for promotion, transfer or training;

(e) dismissal and other detriment (including sexual or racial harassment which can be shown to disadvantage someone in the course of their work).

Recruitment arrangements

Employers commonly require applicants to go through a first sift, to reduce numbers. You will be vulnerable to a complaint of discrimination if this is done in a haphazard way. For example, tribunals have found that arbitrary residence requirements are indirectly discriminatory (*Hussein* v. *Saints Complete House Furnishers* 1979) if they exclude more people from ethnic minority areas.

Practical point: If your company imposes a residence requirement for short-listing, look at why it is imposed and whether you have waived it for other recruits.

Other arrangements found to be discriminatory are when applications from women or ethnic minorities have been given an additional screening, for example by an area manager who wanted to 'vet' them to ensure their acceptability. You cannot defend such arrangements by arguing that they were not intended to discriminate, if the effect was to place an additional hurdle before women or ethnic minority candidates. Nor can your escape by showing that these candidates would not have been selected because they were unsuitable.

Practical point: Make sure all candidates' applications are treated in a similar manner, if there are any differences (e.g. because of the unavailability of staff), make sure that there are no patterns of decisions against one group or one sex.

Differences in interviewing questions have also been found to be discriminatory. For example, in *Makiya* v. *London Borough of Haringay* [1990] a tribunal found sex discrimination because an employer asked a woman candidate her views on how she would deal with reactionary male teachers. This, said the tribunal, assumed that she would find it difficult to deal with these male staff. The correct approach would be to ask all candidates how they have dealt with such problems.

Practical point: Make sure your interview questions relate to the ability to carry out certain tasks, and are applied to all candidates. This does not mean that you have to inflexibly ask the *same* questions. It means that you must not ask them in a way which assumes that women or ethnic minority candidates will be less reliable, or face more difficulties (see Chapter 5).

SELECTION
The most common findings of discrimination made against employers are inferred from:

- applying criteria subjectively, inconsistently or haphazardly;
- making assumptions usually based on stereotypes or prejudice;
- applying an acceptability criteria (on race or sex grounds).

INCONSISTENCIES
For example, in *Camara* v. *London Borough of Barking and Dagenham* [1989], the tribunal found that the council's arrangements for short-listing were unreliable, because the criteria were not applied consistently.

In *Pettit* v. *MEB* (November 1989), the tribunal found discrimination against a woman applicant for stores and distribution supervision. She was not short-listed because she lacked experience of supervising industrial staff. But this criterion was not applied to male applicants.

In *Christopher* v. *BBC* [1988], the tribunal found that the interviewer did not pursue questions about a black applicant's interests and experience of camera work in the same depth as with other candidates, and inferred that this was because of race.

Practical point: Check whether criteria such as qualifications and length of experience have been evenly applied. For example, if you want three years experience; have you excluded anyone with this experience and why? Is there a discriminatory pattern in the way such variations were made?

MAKING ASSUMPTIONS; STEREOTYPING AND PREJUDICE
In *Makiya* v. *London Borough of Haringay* [1990], the tribunal found that the interviews had assumed that Ms Makiya would find it more

difficult to cope with reactionary male employers. The correct approach is to find out how any person has tackled difficult or resistant employees.

In *Killian* v. *Boots the Chemist Ltd* [1990], a tribunal found that the personnel manager discriminated against Mrs Killian when he rejected her, as she had come from Northern Ireland, because he believed all the Irish were the same. They became homesick and returned home.

Practical points: Stereotypes are often based on past experience, but it is unlawful to apply such generalised assumptions. Each applicant has to be assessed according to facts about his or her work, experience and conduct. In this example, the employer could have rejected the candidate if in fact she had a poor work record, but his explanation would have been doubted if he had referred to her national origins. Make sure your staff understand how to avoid their own stereotypes influencing their decisions (see Chapter 5).

Make sure interviewers are trained to assess facts and that they never make assumptions. Carry out spot checks of decisions to see whether they are backed by facts.

APPLYING ACCEPTABILITY CRITERIA

In *Noone* v. *North West Thames Regional Health Authority* [1985] the tribunal found that Dr Noone had suffered racial discrimination when she was not appointed as a consultant microbiologist. One of the reasons given by the respondents for selecting a less well-qualified male candidate was that she was 'not right' and they were unhappy about her 'fitting in'. The tribunal commented that 'it may well be that the [chief medical officer] would have preferred a consultant from Roedean or Westminster School rather than Sri Lanka', and concluded that she would not have been treated in this way if she had been English.

Practical point: You can legitimately take into account a candidate's attributes or experience (but only if these are identified objectively and not assumed) in relation to the balance of skills and attributes in the team with which he or she will work.

You cannot take into account race or sex. In this example, the employers' reasons for the lack of 'fit' were not based on any objective facts about the applicant, they were vague intuitive judgements, which led the tribunal to infer that her race was the reason for her unacceptability.

Access to promotion and training

Similar pitfalls to those listed for recruitment arrangements can arise in access to promotion and training. Tribunals have found unlawful discrimination by employers who have applied selection criteria inconsistently or subjectively, or who have based decisions on stereotyped attitudes. Experience and career progression also become more relevant.

In *Harvett* v. *Humberside Ambulance Service* [1990], a tribunal found discrimination when Ms Harvett was rejected allegedly because of doubts about here ability to cope under pressure. This judgement was made subjectively, not based on any objective record of her work and conduct. The tribunal concluded that in the absence of any evidence about how she carried out her duties, she was 'judged by her gender'.

Practical point: Assessments must be based on facts about tasks done.

In *Sharma* v. *East Midlands Gas* [1988], the tribunal inferred that Mrs Sharma suffered racial discrimination. The selection board preferred two white candidates without qualifications or relevant experience because they displayed flexibility, common sense and capability to learn, whereas Mrs Sharma met their criteria, she had the educational qualifications and supervisory experience, but lacked an 'outgoing personality'.

Practical point: Although personal attributes can be taken into account, they must be balanced against other criteria and applied consistently. In the *East Midlands Gas* case, the choice of two white candidates did not seem justified by these standards.

In *Pratt* v. *Walsall Health Authority* [1988], the tribunal found that the applicant suffered indirect racial discrimination because the authority required 'demonstrated progression' in the nursing career (that is a widespread of experience as well as progress). The tribunal decided that this excluded proportionately more ethnic minority people, and was unjustified because there were other means of assessing potential, at interview or otherwise. The tribunal criticised the authority for failing to apply short-listing criteria consistently; for failing to record criteria to be applied; for failing to keep a record of criteria and reasons for rejecting candidates; for a lack of training and failure to tell staff about their equal opportunities policy.

Practical point: Once again, selection criteria should be identified from a job analysis, and candidates should be notified. Staff involved should have been trained in bias-free selection. Criteria should be applied consistently.

This case illustrates the need for career development and performance appraisal systems. With the aid of these, managers would have made sure that their staff have broad-based career postings and training which would help them advance to higher levels.

In *Sharma* v. *Department of Employment* (1988), the tribunal found that Mr Sharma has suffered racial discrimination by being denied training and being withdrawn from a supervisory role. The tribunal decided that Mr Sharma had been unjustly criticised for his performance which was not based on facts, and removed from supervisory duties after petty complaints from junior staff. Management made no attempt to reinforce his authority, and no attempt to give him management or supervisory training. Mr Sharma had complained of racial discrimination for four years, but nothing had been done about these complaints, because his manager was afraid to inflame matters. The tribunal was critical of this manager's lack of action, which eventually led to Mr Sharma's complete isolation.

Practical point: Performance assessments must be based on facts. If your staff are being criticised by their managers, make sure this is valid criticism. Consider how these weaknesses can be tackled through training. Do not ignore complaints about discrimination; this will simply allow a build up of resentment. Find out about the reason, and counsel staff who are behaving unfairly towards ethnic minority colleagues.

Dismissals and other detriment

Many tribunals decisions have found racial and sexual abuse in relevant circumstances to be a detriment and less favourable treatment.

In *Strathclyde Regional Council* v. *Porcelli* [1986], the court found that sexual harassment was a degrading and unacceptable form of treatment. In *De Souza* v. *Automobile Association* [1986], it was found that for racial harassment to be a detriment, the victim must be disadvantaged in his or her work. The insulting or offensive behaviour must be directed towards the woman or racial minority person, and likely to upset or disturb. The use of a racially offensive remark about Mrs De Souza was not made to her, nor was she intended to hear it. In *Straker* v. *McDonalds' Hamburgers Ltd* [1989], a tribunal found that the employers' failure to investigate a complaint of racial abuse was unlawful; and in *Robinson* v. *Inner City Office Products Ltd* [1989], the tribunal ruled that the employer must act to protect employees from racial abuse, even though she had not formally complained.

A similar finding was made by a tribunal in *Johnson* v. *Gateway Food Markets* [1990], in ruling the employer had breached the Sex Discrimination Act, by failing to train managers to deal with sexual harassment; and failing to provide support and protection for employees.

Practical points: Make sure you have a clear procedure for dealing with cases of harassment and abuse. Train managers so that they know how to deal with cases. Make sure incidents are dealt with promptly and effectively. Check that your procedure is working by reviewing cases already dealt with (see Chapter 10).

Part-time employees

In *Kidd* v. *DRG (UK)* (1985) the Employment Appeal Tribunal found that it was indirect discrimination against women to select part-timers for redundancy before full-time workers. In an earlier case, *Holmes* v. *The Home Office* [1984], it was held that a requirement to work full-time was indirect discrimination against Ms Holmes, as the employer had failed to show that the requirement was justifiable. More significantly, the European Court has ruled in *Rinner-Kuhn* v. *FWW* that all part-time workers were entitled to access to a German employer's sick pay scheme, as failure to allow access would disproportionately exclude women.

Practical points: Flexible working arrangements are an essential part of an equal opportunity programme (see Chapter 8). Make sure that part-time workers and people who have had career breaks are considered for career development or for promotion or training on the same basis as full-time staff. Make sure that flexible working opportunities are available at all levels and in all jobs. Challenge or query any manager who claims that his or her department cannot accommodate flexible working.

Pregnancy and maternity leave

The European Court of Justice (in *Dekker* v. *VJV* (1991)) ruled that it was direct discrimination, and against the EC Equal Treatment Directive, to refuse to offer Ms Dekker a post of training instructor on the grounds of her pregnancy. The employer could not claim that the refusal was justified by the financial consequences of absence due to maternity leave. Another European Court of Justice case in 1991 (*Herz* v. *Aldi Marked*) held that a woman was protected by the Equal Treatment Directive from dismissal because of absence during pregnancy or on maternity leave.

Practical points: These ECJ decisions strengthen the case for introducing flexible working arrangements. Make sure your managers know about the implications and are clear that refusals to employ or dismissals because of pregnancy are unlawful.

Employers' liability

How do you show that your company has done enough to escape liability for discriminatory acts by your staff? Industrial tribunals have used the Equal Opportunity Commission and Commission for Racial Equality Codes of Practice to help them assess whether an employer has done enough to ensure that equal opportunity policy is effective.

Training

In *Carney* v. *Bass Mitchells Butler Ltd* [1989], the tribunal found that the employer was not liable for an employee's racial discrimination, because he had been given a six-hour training session on employment law, followed by a refresher course. He had also been given copies of the company's policy.

In *Batters* v. *Bolivar Stamping* [1989], the tribunal found that the company (part of the Delta Group) had not done enough to prevent their staff discriminating. The company had posted their equal opportunity policy in the workplace, and the manager concerned had had an hour-long induction course which included the equal opportunity policy. The tribunal described this as 'the minimum'.

In another case, *Jalota* v. *Commissioners of Inland Revenue* [1990], the tribunal warned the Inland Revenue that it would not have escaped liability because, although they had a 'prolific outpouring of notes and brochures ... they are asked to take steps ... to promote the policy. In their efforts to do so, they remained too passive.'

Practical points: Training and guidance specific to each job is needed. You must also have a system which defines a manager's objectives and monitors performance against these.

CHECKLIST

Avoiding race and sex discrimination is the responsibility of all managers of staff, and all those involved in recruitment. Your first action must be to make sure that your staff:

- know how to behave in a non-discriminatory way;
- know the common pitfalls and how to avoid them.

As a manager, you need to check that your system is working. To do this you need to:

- monitor results of decisions;
- pick up discrepancies and differences with a pattern of race or sex-bias;
- find out the reasons for these differences;
- are there rules or conditions or decisions which can be changed to reduce differences? Or are the rules or criteria being misapplied?

APPENDIX 1

Cases cited: chapter 12

1. Khanna v. Ministry of Defence. 1981 IRLR 331 EAT.
2. Chattopadhyay v. The Headmaster of Holloway School. 1981 IRLR 487 EAT.
3. Jones v. Chief Adjudication Officer 1990 IRLR 533 CA.
4. Hussein v. Saints Complete House Furnishers 1979 IRLR 337.
5. Makiya v. London Borough of Haringey 1990 IT 03023/89/.
6. Camara v. London Borough of Barking and Dagenham 1989 IT 12420/89.
7. Pettit v. MEB 1989 IT 8353/89.
8. Christopher v. BBC 1988 IT 22338/87 (London).
9. Killian v. Boots the Chemist Ltd 1990 IT 11079/89.
10. Noone v. North West Thames Regional Health Authority 1988 IRLR 195 CA.
11. Harvatt v. Humberside Ambulance Service 1990 IT 3907/90.
12. Sharma v. East Midlands Gas 1988 IT 09018/85 and 04968/87 (Leicester).
13. Pratt v. Walsall Health Authority 1987 IT 36145/86 (Birmingham).
14. Sharma v. Department of Employment 1988 IT 15047/87 (Liverpool).
15. Strathclyde Regional Council v. Porcelli 1986 IRLR 134 CS.
16. De Souza v. The Automobile Association 1986 IRLR 103 CA.
17. Straker v. MacDonalds Hamburgers Ltd 1989 IT 18273/88.
18. Robinson v. Inter City Office Products Ltd 1989 IT 4039/89.
19. Johnson v. Gateway Food Markets 1990 IT 4079/90.
20. Kidd v. DRG (UK) 1985 IRLR 190 EAT.
21. The Home Office v. Holmes 1984 IRLR 299 EAT.

22. Rinner-Kuhn v. F.W.W. Spezial – Gebandereinigung Gmbh 1989 IRLR 178 ECJ.
23. Dekker v. Stichting Vorming Scentrum voor Jonge Volwassenen (v JV Centrum) Plus November 1990 IRLR ECJ.
24. Herz v. Aldi Marked k/s November 1990 ECJ.
25. Carney v. Bass Mitchells Butler Ltd 1989 IT 19708/88.
26. Batters v. Bolivar Stamping 1989 IT 3966/89.
27. Jalota v. Commissioners of Inland Revenue 1990 (IT/90).

APPENDIX 2

Useful addresses

Official agencies and sources of advice

For publications & advice on implementing equal opportunity programmes

Equal Opportunities Commission
Overseas House
Quay Street
Manchester
M3 3HN

061-833-9244

Commission for Racial Equality
Elliot House
10/12 Allington Street
London
SW1E 5EH

(Also for advice on contact with race equality councils.)

071-828-7022

Race Relations Employment Advisory Service
Steel House
Tothill Street
London
SW1

071-834-6644

Employment Service's Sheltered Employment Branch
Sheltered Employment Branch
Steel City House
c/o Moorfoot
Sheffield
S1 4PQ

0742-739190

Other agencies

Institute of Personnel Management (IPM)
IPM House
Camp Road
London SW19 4UX

081-946-9100

Institute of Manpower Studies (IMS)
Mantell Buildings
University of Sussex
Falmer
Brighton
BN1 9RF

The Windsor Fellowship
c/o Citibank
336 Strand
London
WC2R 1HB

071-438-1056

A programme of training and sponsorship aimed at linking undergraduates, especially those from ethnic minorities, with major employers.

PATH Yorkshire Ltd
Dyson's Building
Buslington Lane
Leeds
LS7 2DB

0532-624600

Positive action training for professional
and career opportunities for ethnic
minorities.

Project COMTRAN Ltd
Oakwell House
8 Oak Avenue
Bradford
BD8 7AQ

0274–547330

Positive action training for ethnic
minorities for access to management and
careers.

Womens Returners' Network
c/o Ruth Michaels
Hatfield Polytechnic
College Lane
Hatfield
Herts

Keeping in touch with other returners.

Women in Science and Engineering
(WISE)
c/o The Engineering Council
10 Maltravers Street
London
WC2

071-240-7891

Encourages girls and women to consider
science and engineering careers.

National Childminding Association
8 Masons Hill
Bromley
Kent
BR2 9EY

081-464-6164

Advice on setting up childminding
schemes.

Women in Management
64 Marryat Road
London
SW19 5BN

081-946-1238

Promotion and development of women to
management.

Workplace Nurseries Campaign
77 Holloway Road
London
N7 8JZ

071–700–0821

Advice on setting up nurseries.

Gingerbread
35 Wellington Street
London
WC2E 7BN

071-240-0953

National Children's Bureau
(Under Fives Unit)
8 Wakely Street
London
EC1V 7QE

Pre-School Playgroups Association
61–63 Kings Cross Road
London
WC1X 9LL

071-833-0991

National Association for Maternal and
Child Welfare
1 South Audley Street
London
W1Y 6JS

071-491-1315 (Educational Department)
071-491-2772

National Children's Play and Recreation
Unit
359–361 Euston Road
London
NW1 3AL

071-383-5455

National Out of School Alliance
Oxford House
Derbyshire Street
Bethnal Green Road
London
E2 6HG

071-739-4878

National Playing Fields Association
25 Ovington Square
London
SW3 1LQ

071-584-6445

European Women's Development
Network
Rue Washington
40-B1050 Brussels

(02) 648.03.85

Advice on disability

British Rheumatism and Arthritis
Association
5 Grosvenor Crescent
London
SW1X 7ER

081-235-0902

Multiple Sclerosis Society
25 Essie Road
Fulham
London
SW6 1EE

071-736-6267

National Association for Mental Health
22 Harley Street
London
W1N 2ED

071-637-0741

Royal Association for Disability and
Rehabilitation
25 Mortimer Street
London
W1N 8AB

071-637-5400

Royal National Institute for the Blind
224 Great Portland Street
London
W1N 6AA

071-387-8033

Royal National Institute for the Deaf
105 Gower Street
London
WC1E 6AH

071-387-8033

The Spastics Society
12 Park Crescent
London
W1N 3EQ

071-636-5020

The Spinal Injuries Association
Yeomans House
St James' Lane
London
N10 3DF

081-444-2121

Disabled Living Foundation (DLF)
380–384 Harrow Road
London
W9 2HY

071-289-6111

Outset
Drake House
18 Creekside
London
SE8 3DZ

081-692-7141

Shaw Trust
Caithness House
Western Way
Melksham
Wiltshire
SN12 8DZ

0225-790860

Association of Spina Bifida and
Hydrocephalus
Suite 7, Staniland Court
Staniland Way
Werrington
Peterborough
PE4 6RY

0733-321818

British Epilepsy Association
Anstey House
40 Hanover Square
Leeds
LS3 1BE

0532 439393

Link Employment
54 Blyth Road
London
W14 0HA

Royal Society for Mentally Handicapped
Children and Adults (MENCAP)
169a City Road
Cardiff
CF2 3JB

Some sources of training material

BNA Communications Inc
3439 Key West Avenue
Rockville, Maryland 20850-9989
USA

800-233-6067

Equal Employment Opportunity training
material from the USA.
(Also available from: Synoposia: 1 Frimley
Road, Camberley, Surrey 0276-26172)

Melrose Film Productions Ltd
16 Bromwells Road
London
SW4 0BL

Training video: 'The Tale of "O"'.
(Also available from Commission for
Racial Equality.)

MAST Learning Systems
MLS 26 Warwick Road
London
SW5 9UD

Inter-active computer package on the
Equal Opportunity at work: Questions
and answers on the EO legislation.

Commission for Racial Equality
Videos on the legislation: and Equal
Opportunities:

'Strategies for employment': BBC/OU
Video on E.O. Strategy.
'Recruiting for Quality': BBC/OU Video
on recruitment.

BBC Enterprises Ltd
Education and Training Sales
Woodlands 80 Wood Lane
London
W12 0TT

081-743-5588

A range of equal opportunity videos
including 'Women in Management' and
'Black'.

Concord Films Council
201 Felixstone Road
Ipswich
Suffolk
IP3 9BJ

Videos include 'The Eye of the Storm' and 'A Class Divided' (valuable insights into race discrimination through exercises by Yale University Films) and 'The Deaf Manager'.

Centre for Staff Development in Higher Education
2 Taviton Street
London
WC1H 0BT

071-380-0599

Trigger videos on equal opportunities in employment: 'Through a Hundred Pairs of Eyes'.

Employment Service (from the Disablement Advisory Service)
'It Worked Fine – Managing Disabled People.'

'It Can be Done'.

'Damaged not Daft'.
CSL Vision
PO Box 35
Wetherby
Yorks
LS23 7EX

0937-541010

London Boroughs Disability Resource Team (LBDRT)
'More Than Just a Fine Sounding Slogan'. Trigger Video

LBDRT
Bedford House
125–133 Camden High Street
London
NW1 7JR

071-482-5299

OMCS
'Lets be Fair'.
Available from:
Central Office of Information
Hercules Road
London SE1

The Spastics Society
'Stand Up the Real Glynn Vernon'.
Vision
Park Hall Road Trading Estate
London
SE21 8E1

081-761-3035

APPENDIX 3

Bibliography

Legislation

Disabled Person's (Employment) Act 1944

Sex Discrimination Act 1975

Race Relations Act 1976

Companies Act 1985

Children Act 1989

Equal Pay Act 1970

Data protection Act 1984

Employment Protection (Consolidation) Act 1978

Codes of practice

CRE 1984 Code of Practice: For the elimination of racial discrimination and the promotion of equality of opportunity in employment.

EOC 1984 Code of Practice: For the elimination of discrimination on the ground of sex and marriage and the promotion of equal opportunity in employment.

Department of Employment (1988) Code of Good Practice on the employment of people with a disability.

Statistics

1981 Census/1991 Census – Available in

County Reports or Local Statistics from: Office of Population Censuses and Surveys, St Catherine's House WC2B 6JP.

Men and Women in Britain – annual publication by EOC.

Labour Force Survey – Extracts published in the monthly 'Employment Gazette' by Employment Department.

Universities Central Council on Admissions (UCCA): Graduate Destinations: annual publication.

Journals

Equal Opportunities Review (EOR): published by Industrial Relations Services, 18–20 Highbury Place, London NW5 1QP.

Personnel Today, published by Reed Business Publishing, Quadrant House, The Quadrant, Sutton, Surrey SM2 5AS.

Industrial Relations Law Reports (IRLR): published by Industrial Relations Services.

Books/reports

The Dignity of Women at Work (1988) – Michael Rubenstein, EEC.

Women and Harassment at Work (1983) – Natalie Hadjifotiou, Pluto Press.

Employers Guide to Disability (1986) – M. Kettle and B. Massie, Royal Association for Disability and Rehabilitation.

An equal chance for disabled people? A study of discrimination in employment (1986) E. Fry, Spastics Society.

CRE (1987) – Chartered Accountancy Training Contracts: Report of Formal Investigation into ethnic minority recruitment.

CRE (1998) – Racial Discrimination and Grievance Procedures.

CRE (1989) – Indirect Discrimination in employment. A practical guide.

CRE (1987) – Training: the implementation of equal opportunities at work, Vols. 1 and 2.

Training for Equality Vol. 3 (1991).

The employers guide to childcare: Working Mothers Association.

Discrimination: A guide to relevant case laws on Race and Sex Discrimination and Equal Pay – Michael Rubenstein, Eclipse Publication 1991.

Equal Opportunities: A Directory of Trainers, Consultants and Training, Material from the NHS Training Authority, St Bartholomews Court, 18 Christmas Street, Bristol BS1 5BT.

How to organise a holiday play scheme, National Playing Fields Association (revised 1988).

Insurance for children's play, National Playing Fields Association, second ed., 1987.

Legal responsibility, Nick Madge and Jan Loxley. The National Out of School Alliance.

The Employer's Guide to Childcare, Working Mother's Association, 1989.

Finding and choosing day care for your under fives VOLCUF and the National Consumer Council, 1988.

New Mothers at Work – employment and childcare, Julia Brannen and Peter Moss. Unwin paperbacks, 1988.

Working with Children: developing a curriculum in the early years, Drummond, Lally and Pugh. National Children's Bureau (Under Fives Unit), 1989).

Index

acceptability criteria 189–90
accountability
  departmental 25
  individual 25–7
action programmes 29–31, 33
applicants, job *see* job applicants
appraisals, performance 12, 26–7, 97–9
assessment, bases for
  aptitude tests 79
  experience 77–8
  in-tray exercises 87–8
  interviews 78–9, 83–7
  job simulations 87
  qualifications 77–8
  tests, use of 88–91
assumptions, unconscious 9–10, 188
attitudes
  assumptions, unconscious 9–10, 188
  cross-cultural behavioural differences 10–11
  preferences, perceived staff/customer 8–9
  prejudice 7–8
  stereotyping 8, 188

behavioural patterns *see* attitudes
benefits of programme 2, 182–3
biodata 82–3
Blueline Metropolitan Buses 104–5

careers
  breaks, long-term 140–3
  development 93–106
  services, links with 68–70
case studies, subjects of
  complaint of discrimination 14–15
  promotion interview 104–5

qualifications for job 78
training 73–4
childcare
after-school care 148
arrangements 143–6
childminder service 146–7, 152
nurseries 148–50
playschemes 150–2
vouchers 147, 152
civil service 65–6
Commission for Racial Equality 170, 193
communities, ethnic minorities, links with 70–1
Companies Act (1985) 155, 164
company profiles, building of 51–63
complaints
case study 14–15
dealing with 14
of racial and sexual discrimination 167–70
at industrial tribunals 185–6
learning from 13
of racial and sexual harassment 174–7
construction industry
ethnic minorities in 66, 73
women in 66, 72–3
consultation 35–6, 41
costs of programme 179–81
cross-cultural behavioural differences 10–11
customers
perceived preferences of 8–9
serving of 71–2

Data Protection Act (1984) 44
Dignity of Women at Work, The (Rubenstein) 172
Disabled Persons (Employment) Act (1944) 39, 46, 47, 154, 164
disabilities, people with *see also* discrimination
analysis of monitoring data re. 51–4
buildings, access to 156–8
classification of 48–9
collection of monitoring data re. 46–7
consultation with 35–6, 41
definition of term 47
and Department of Employment 161
distribution of, in employment 4
employers' legal obligations 154–8
equipment at workplace for 158–59
home-working 136–7
interpretation of monitoring data re. 54–6
and labour market in 1990s 1
and positive action training 122–29

recruitment of 11–12, 65–75, 77–91, 187–8
registration of 154–5
Remote Working Scheme 137
sheltered placements for 137–8
voluntary organisations for 162–4
Disablement Advisory Service 137–8, 161
Disablement Resettlement Officer 161
discrimination
complaints of 13–15, 167–70
direct 5
and employers' positive action 5–6
indirect 5, 76–7
and industrial tribunals 185–6
recognising 13, 169

education services, links with 68–70
employer *see* equal opportunity employer
Employment and Handicap (Prescott-Clarke) 48
Employment Rehabilitation Service 161, 162
Equal Opportunity Commission 193
equal opportunity employer 1–3, 4, 7
equal opportunity policy
audit re. 21–2
economic benefits of 2, 181–3
Ford Motor Co statement 19–21
and harassment, racial and sexual 174
implementation of 33–36
Leicester City Council statement 18–19
Littlewoods code of practice 31–3, 106
statements, usefulness of 17–18
TSB Group statement 18
Equal Pay Act (1970) 187
equality, barriers to 7
in promoting staff 93–5, 190–1
in selecting staff 62–3, 65, 76–9
and working environment 166
equality of opportunity, meaning of 4
ethnic minorities *see also* discrimination
action on monitoring data re. 57–63
analysis of monitoring data re. 51–4
and assumptions, unconscious 9–10
and behavioural differences 10–11
career development of 12, 99–106
classification of, per CRE 49–50
collection of monitoring data re. 49–50
communities, links with 70–1
in construction industry 66, 73
consultation with 35–6, 41
definition of terms 6

distribution of, in employment 4
harassment, racial 170–7
interpretation of monitoring data re. 54–7
and labour market in 1990s 1, 2
and positive action training 123–29
and preferences, perceived staff/customer 8–9
prejudice against 7–8, 189
promotion of 12, 99–106
recruitment of 11–12, 65–75, 77–91, 187–8
selection of 12, 77–91, 188
stereotyping of 8, 189
European Community
  Commission's action programme (1991–5) 3
  Commission's Social Charter 155–6
  and disabilities, people with 155–6
  Equal Treatment Directive 193–4
  and equal treatment requirements 4–5
  and sexual harassment 171–2, 173
examples, subjects of
  code of practice 30–2, 106
  objectives, company/group 24–5
  policy statements 18–21
  positive action training schemes 127–8

'fast-track development' 12, 103
financial aspects of programme 2, 179–83
'Fit for Work' scheme 25
flexible working pattern
  career breaks, long-term 140–3
  childcare arrangements 143–52
  description of 131–2
  home-working 135–7
  introduction of 132, 138–9
  job sharing 135–6
  parental leave 139–40
  part-time working 135–6, 192
  sheltered placements 137–8
  term-time working 135–6
  working hours, flexible 133–5
Ford Motor Company 19–21
'four-fifths rule' 56–7, 59

'glass ceiling' 94–5, 123
Graduate Careers Advisory Services, Association of (AGCAS) 66

Handicap, Employment and (Prescott-Clarke) 48
harassment, sexual and racial 170–7
Helios programmes 155
home-working 135–7

industrial tribunals 185–6
interviews
  case study 104–5
  job applicants' 78–9, 83–7
  for promotion 100–1

job analysis 80–1
job applicants
  attracting 67–71
  feedback from 66–7
  form for 82, 83
  interviews of *see* interviews, job applicants
  qualifications and experience of 77–8
  rates of, reasons for low 65–6
  sifting of 77
  testing of 79, 87–91
job sharing 135–6

labour market in 1990s 1–2
Leicester City Council 18–19
Leyland Daf 73–4
liability, employers' 193
Littlewoods Organisation, The 3, 31–3, 106

maternity leave 192–3
mission statements 24–5
monitoring, statistical
  action 60–3
  action areas, identification of 57–60
  analysis of data 51–4
  collection of data *see* statistics for monitoring, collection of
  definition of term 38
  interpretation of data 54–7

NOW *see* Women, New Opportunities for

objectives
  definition of 23–4
  departmental 25
  group/company 24–5
  individual 25–7

parental leave 139–40
part-time working 135–6, 192
personnel management, structure of 33–6
positive action 5–6
  training 123–9
potential, identification of 87, 101–2
preferences, perceived staff/customer 8–9

pregnancy 192–3
prejudice 7–8, 189
promotion 3, 12
  access to 190–1
  barriers to 93–5, 190–1
  case study 104–5
  identification of skills needed 96
  system, operation of 99–106

Race Relations Act
  (1968) 5
  (1976) 4, 5, 6, 187
Racial Discrimination (1965 PEP) 5
Racial Discrimination and Grievance Procedures (CRE) 170
Racial Equality Councils 70
racial harassment 170–7
recruitment of staff 11–12, 65–75, 77–91, 187–8
Remote Working Scheme 137
role models 71
RRA *see* Race Relations Act (1976)

School Leaver Attitudes to Work in the Civil Service, Survey of (SCPR 1986) 65
SDA *see* Sex Discrimination Act (1975)
selection of staff 12, 77–91, 188
Sex Discrimination Act (1975) 4–5, 187
sexual harassment 170–7
sheltered placements 137–8
shortlists 81–2, 86
Single European Market 2
statistics for monitoring, collection of 38–9
  disabilities, people with 46–9
  ethnic origins 49–51
  job applicants 45–6
  recruits 45–6
  staff in post 39–45
stereotyping 8, 189

targets 23–4
  numerical 28–9
  timetable for action 27–8
term-time working 135–6
tests, job applicants' 79, 87–91
trade unions 35–6, 41
trainers, pitfalls for 109–10
training, equal opportunities *see also* positive action
  access to 31–2, 190–1
  components of 110–12
  for harassment, dealing with 177
  and industrial tribunal decisions 193

pitfalls 109–10
planning/setting up 112–22
reason for 108
TSB Group 3, 18

warning signs of inequality 13, 169
women *see also* discrimination
action on monitoring data re. 57–63
analysis of monitoring data re. 51–4
and assumptions, unconscious 9–10
and behavioural differences 10–11
career development of 12, 13, 99–106
in construction industry 66, 72–3
consultation with 35–6
distribution of, in employment 4
harassment, sexual 170–7
interpretation of monitoring data re. 54–7
and labour market in 1990s 1, 2
New Opportunities for (EC) 3
and positive action training 123–29
and preferences, perceived staff/customer 8–9
prejudice against 7–8, 189
promotion of 12, 13, 99–106
recruitment of 11–12, 65–75, 77–91, 187–8
selection of 12, 77–91, 188
stereotyping of 8, 189
Women and Harassment at Work (Hadjifotiou) 172
working hours, flexible 133–5
working pattern *see* flexible working pattern